# LENTEN MEDITATIONS

# LENTEN
# MEDITATIONS

*Post Crucem, Lucem*

REVEREND PETER STRAVINSKAS

NEWMAN HOUSE PRESS
*Mount Pocono   Pennsylvania*

These meditations were offered on Vatican Radio's
live website during Lent 2002.

Cover art: *The Resurrection: Christ steps from the tomb
while the guards sleep,*
mural, Piero della Francesca (1415–1492),
Pinacoteca Comunale, San Sepolcro, Italy.
© Erich Lessing / Art Resource, N.Y.
Used with permission

Published by Newman House Press
21 Fairview Avenue, Mount Pocono PA 18344

ISBN 0–9704022–4–4

*Text composed in Palatino and Felix Titling*

PRINTED IN THE UNITED STATES OF AMERICA

# CONTENTS

## HOLY WEEK

## TRIDUUM AND EASTER

# PREFACE

The popularity of *Advent Meditations: Helps to "Wait in Joyful Hope"* and explicit requests for a Lenten sequel prompted the publication of the present volume. It should also be noted that these meditations were offered on Vatican Radio's live website during Lent 2002 and received a most favorable response, causing us to trust that the reader will have a similar reaction.

Comments about the work's subtitle and cover art may aid in setting the proper frame of reference for entering into these reflections.

*Post crucem, lucem* translates as "after the Cross, the light." It embodies the essence of Christian discipleship. First, it teaches—as did our Lord—that following Him requires a person to carry one's cross. No shirking is possible. Gospels of success and human fulfillment are, at best, incomplete gospels and, at worst, horribly deceptive. Only the individual who takes seriously the Master's invitation to bear the cross can find the level of happiness that makes life truly worth living right now, precisely because it guarantees a life on high with Christ for all eternity. And that brings us to the second part of this spiritual maxim: There *is* light after the Cross; it is not all morbid and depressing. Just as we have Jesus' challenge to bear one's cross, so too we have His solemn promise that a willingness to do so will bring about the best prospects for human flourishing even "in this vale of tears," as well as in Paradise. The repentance and penance of Ash Wednesday lead inexorably and infallibly to genuine Easter joy.

Throughout history, many artists have sought to depict Christ's Passion, Death, and Resurrection. Few have been able to combine all the elements in one work. Piero della Francesca is an exception. In his mural painting "The Resurrection," with the Lord still emerging from the tomb, we see resurrection in progress. With his still-fresh wounds, we can appreciate just how close we are to the events of Good Friday. With His banner emblazoned with the Cross, we are made to realize that "death is swallowed up in victory."

The lovely preface for the Solemnity of the Ascension has us pray: "Where He has gone, we hope to follow." Yes, we hope to take up our personal crosses in union with Him and His Cross, as we hope to share in His glorious Resurrection. We make our own the words of the memorial acclamation: "Lord, by Your Cross and Resurrection, You have set us free. You are the Savior of the world." Yes, our Savior, my Savior.

# ASH WEDNESDAY

*Joel 2:12–18*
*Psalm 51*
*2 Corinthians 5:20–6:2*
*Matthew 6:1–6, 16–18*

It seems strange to many that on the very day that Catholics have traditionally worn ashes on their foreheads, the Church also reads the passage from Matthew's Gospel in which Jesus condemns religious externalism. In reality, however, there is no contradiction. The ashes are a call to repentance and a reminder of our mortality—directed as much to ourselves as to others.

The ashes are not intended as a show of religiosity but as a sobering exhortation to acknowledge our sinfulness and to take advantage of this "acceptable time and day of salvation." If we truly enter the spirit of Lent, we have God's assurance that He will take these ashes and once again breathe His life into them—eternal life.

# THURSDAY
# AFTER
# ASH WEDNESDAY

*Deuteronomy 30:15–20*
*Psalm 1*
*Luke 9:22–25*

God presents us with His laws and says that life comes through obedience. To illustrate that fact, Jesus lives obediently—even unto death, and God keeps His promise by rewarding the obedience of Jesus with life eternal. Today Luke reminds us that the Christian life involves a daily carrying of one's cross, which is another way of looking at obedience to God's Will. Let us use this season to analyze our actions, to purify our motives, and to accept our crosses joyfully. All of this will help us discover what really matters in life.

# FRIDAY
# AFTER
# ASH WEDNESDAY

*Isaiah 58:1–9a*
*Psalm 51*
*Matthew 9:14–15*

Today we hear Jesus say that His disciples will fast when He is gone. Fasting played a very important part in one's Lenten observance years ago; in the modern Church, fasting is pretty much left to our own discretion and devotion.

While fasting may be an optional exercise, penance is not. Each Christian must recognize his sinfulness and decide on how he will make amends. If abstaining from food doesn't move you, try Isaiah's program: "Feed the hungry, care for the weak and afflicted, work to correct injustices." This is both penance and charity—it concretely demonstrates our love for both God and neighbor.

# SATURDAY
# AFTER
# ASH WEDNESDAY

*Isaiah 58:9–14*
*Psalm 86*
*Luke 5:27–32*

Some people feel that Jesus was rather indiscriminate in choosing associates, but He really wasn't. He tells us He does not want the self-righteous—He wants sinners who are convinced of their sinfulness and wish to be saved.

Jesus invites Levi to "follow Him," and we are told that he responded by leaving everything behind. During Lent, the Church invites us to a closer following of Jesus by prayer, self-denial, and works of charity. Lent is a time for sinners to leave behind the excess baggage that slows down our homeward journey.

# WEEK ONE OF LENT

# FIRST SUNDAY

## YEAR A

*Genesis 2:7–9; 3, 1–7*
*Psalm 51*
*Romans 5:12–19*
*Matthew 4:1–11*

Lent is a season of contrasts: sin and grace; feasting and fasting; death and life. The contrast is the most striking when we consider the behavior of the first Adam and the second Adam: The first was tempted and sinned, while the second was tempted but prevailed over His Tempter.

If this holy season is going to make us any holier, it will be through making us come to a deeper and better understanding of temptation. Some basic facts are essential to grasp. First, the Devil is real, and he has an uncanny insight into human psychology, preying on our weaknesses, which he seems to know better than we do ourselves, or at least more than we are usually ready to admit.

Jesus, the Messiah, is thus subjected to three primal enticements (which have a tug on all people), but they had special significance for One Who would be a Savior. His first temptation was from the flesh—carnal desires. Today we see all around us the abuse of sex, food, drugs, and alcohol. This is what happens when the body masters the mind; the human person is enslaved by the idolatry of creature comforts and eroticism.

Christ's second temptation came from the mind, which appeals to pride and envy, among the basest instincts. Today this is operative among people who think that science has all the answers to the questions of life. These short-sighted people fail to realize that science is neutral and requires direction, which can come only from minds and hearts formed by correct moral principles. When man succumbs to the silliness of Adam and Eve—trying to be like God—he invariably becomes the victim of these urges, the just reward for the idolatry of a scientism-gone-wild or a pseudo-intellectualism.

The Lord's final temptation came from things. It gains its influence from the force of greed. Today we feel its power among those who value possessions more than persons. In their foolishness, they never learn that the human heart attains complete fulfillment and happiness only in the Creator and never in the creature. St. Augustine, who had been tempted in every way and had given in to just about every one of those allurements, finally came to the sobering conclusion—after much painful experimentation: "Thou hast made us for Thyself, O Lord, and our hearts are restless until they rest in Thee." The sinner-turned-saint still offers that counsel to those locked in by the idolatry of materialism.

Lent is a time to smash the idols in our lives; it is a crash course in confronting temptation. How does one respond appropriately to this phenomenon? Granted, massive doses of actual grace can be infused by Almighty God when the Devil makes his assaults. Generally, however, the Church expects us to prepare for temptation by good Christian living on a daily, on-going basis.

Lent is an opportunity to do intensively what should be done normally. Works of prayer, charity, and self-denial should be embraced with gusto as ways of demonstrating our love for God and as means of strengthening ourselves for the battle of temptation. When the hour of testing comes—and it always does (sometimes far more often than we wish)—the good Lents of our lives will have provided us with the good habits and necessary experience to handle temptation effectively, which is to say, we shall know how to tell the Devil to go to hell!

The Church is most realistic in assessing human nature: Temptation is inevitable; sin is not. St. Augustine again sets the pace for us by reminding us that in Christ's temptation, we were all tempted. Fair enough, but there's more: In Christ's victory over temptation, we were all victorious. That, then, enables us to face the temptations embodied in Lent with a sense of confidence and even joy. Lent is a prelude to Easter; it is the time of fasting to prepare for the feasting; it is the transition from sin to grace; it is the hour of death leading to everlasting life— all done in and through the Christ Who observed the first Lent by spending forty days in the desert.

# FIRST SUNDAY

## YEAR B

*Genesis 9:8–15*
*Psalm 25*
*1 Peter 3:18–22*
*Mark 1:12–15*

Imagine, if you will, a desert: arid, lifeless, boring in its sameness, oppressive in its heat, removed from civilization, inhabited by wild beasts, eerie because of the possibilities for violence, where suffering and death seem so real. In fact, the Jews believed that the desert was the abode of evil spirits. And yet, Mark tells us that Jesus is driven into the desert under the impulse of the Spirit.

Here, Jesus does battle with the forces of evil—ushering in the last days, when the final contest between good and evil will take place. Mark maintains a remarkable silence on what happens during these forty days; we know only that Jesus emerges stronger and more confident than ever of His mission.

The history of humanity is the story of God's continuing effort to establish and maintain contact with us; that is the whole point of the First Reading. Jesus' temptation—and, later, His death, is a further proof of this. Jesus enters into the whole human condition, tainted and sinful as it is. That is why the exhortation in the Second Reading makes such sense: Jesus suffered, so we should expect to suffer; but Jesus also triumphed, so we should expect to triumph, too!

Having painted such a grim picture of life in the desert, I should also note that there is something different about this particular desert. In spite of the potential for violence in the Gospel scene, we also have a sense of peace. Although Jesus is with the wild beasts, we have no fear for Him. Nor does Jesus appear to be mastered by the elements; He seems in control throughout. Is there a hint here that the sinful, disordered condition of our world is now being renewed? Do we have here a hint of a "Paradise Restored"?

Sin breeds hate and discord, even in nature. Grace produces harmony and order. Jesus comes proclaiming a time of fulfillment—a time when God's reign will be established in men's hearts. "Reform your lives and believe in the good news!" Jesus says that after going through the depths of human suffering and temptation. Jesus has the right to make this kind of proclamation because He knows that it is possible to overcome temptation. He has done it, and so can we. Reform is possible. Our situation is not hopeless; we are meant to be greater and better than we are. That is the good news Jesus brings, and that is the good news Lent bids us practice.

# FIRST SUNDAY

## YEAR C

*Deuteronomy 26:4–10*
*Psalm 91*
*Romans 10:8–13*
*Luke 4:1–13*

So many words and messages bombard us each day with their empty promises that we tend to turn off all the forms of verbal communication we encounter. That is especially sad because we run the risk of missing out on some truly valuable communiques. As men and women who stand in the Judaeo-Christian Tradition, we can never forget the deep importance attached to a word and its power in both the Old and New Testaments. Creation took place by God's Word; hope for salvation was offered through a word passed down through the centuries. John identifies Jesus as nothing less than God's personal Word to mankind. In our modern world we do need to be selective in the words we accept, but we should never be tempted to put aside or disregard God's Word revealed to us in the Scriptures.

In the First Reading we heard the recital of a primitive creed professing God's abiding presence with the Hebrew nation. That word of faith was also a word of hope, especially in times of national disaster, when the people had to be reassured of God's love and concern for them. Even when the Temple as God's earthly dwelling among

His people was destroyed, the Hebrews held to the Scriptures as a source of divine presence and inspiration. It is in that light that Jesus is seen as a most devout Jew—in the midst of anxiety, mental torment, and temptation—turning to the Scriptures for strength to be faithful to His mission, a most dramatic witness to His love and reverence for the Scriptures. In all the circumstances of His life, Jesus demonstrated the necessity for a person of faith to be in touch with the powerful message God's Word provides—in times of doubt and crisis, as well as in moments of joy.

Jesus' Sermon on the Mount is a basic restatement of the values of peace, love, and harmony contained in the Old Testament. His calling people to conversion of heart was a call first issued by the prophets hundreds of years earlier. Faithful to the Word of the Scriptures throughout His life, He was faithful to them until the end, as He relied on the words of the Psalms to express His own confusion and inner turmoil on the Cross.

If Jesus took inspiration from the Scriptures, shouldn't we follow His example? The Second Vatican Council actively encouraged Catholics to read the Bible, reversing a trend of centuries during which the Church feared that misreading could cause more serious problems than not reading at all. The Church is now sufficiently confident that we have a well-educated laity that could tremendously benefit from the exposure to Scripture. Have you taken up the challenge?

If you haven't, then Lent would be an ideal time to do something about it. This season could be an opportune moment in your life to grow in an understanding and appreciation of God's Word. I am not talking about embarking upon a simple theoretical or academic exercise; nor am I talking about developing that happy fundamentalist technique of having thousands of apt biblical quotations at your fingertips. What I am suggesting is that you begin a program of prayer and study that will put you in touch with the power of the Scriptures to change your life at the very practical level of daily living. Take the Word to heart, live by it, and become that Word for others.

Reading the Bible is not like reading the latest bestselling novel. For the experienced person, it is hard work, requiring genuine devotion and no small amount of determination. Involve yourself in formal courses and lectures (offered as a part of most parish adult education programs) as a way of deepening your knowledge of the Bible and the biblical world. Read books and articles on the subject. And then put all of that necessary background information to work by a faithful, daily reading of the Scriptures. During this Lenten season, why not commit yourself to a prayerful reading of the Gospels for fifteen minutes each day? It is a manageable project that could surely unite you more closely to the Lord during these forty days; it may also develop into a habit that would spill over into your "post-Lenten" life.

# MONDAY

## WEEK I

*Leviticus 19:1–2, 11–18*
*Psalm 19*
*Matthew 25:31–46*

As the Lord gives His commandments, He also gives His reasons: That by following His way, we will become holy. Many people have strange ideas about holiness that have nothing to do with God's ideas on the subject.

Holiness is right living, being at peace with God and neighbor. Jesus sees the two as so related that He tells us that what we do for or against our neighbor is done to Him. Let us try to become holy by tending to the needs of the Christ Who lives and suffers among us.

# TUESDAY

## WEEK I

*Isaiah 55:10–11*
*Psalm 34*
*Matthew 6:7–15*

Jesus taught His disciples only one prayer, and it is a real stumbling-block for many of us because we have been told to pray it—but so often we don't mean it. ". . . Thy Kingdom come." His Kingdom will come when we treat others with justice, with mercy, with love; when we conform our thoughts to His. "Thy will be done." His Will will be done when we place our lives in His hands and trust in His fatherly love. ". . . Forgive us our trespasses as we forgive . . ." God forbid that He should ever do that—for we are so resentful, so bent on revenge, so slow to forgive. Let's try to change our attitudes so that we can say this prayer with the sincerity it requires.

# WEDNESDAY

## WEEK I

*Jonah 3:1–10*
*Psalm 51*
*Luke 11:29–32*

A pagan city is visited by an itinerant preacher and is converted—while religious people fail to respond to a call for repentance.

Isn't that frequently the situation today? We believers have a way of thinking we are guaranteed salvation just because we bear the name of Christian. But our failure to respond to people's needs shows that we are not true believers. We must listen to the demands of the Gospel afresh—for they come from One greater than Jonah.

# THURSDAY

## WEEK I

*Esther 14:1, 3–5, 12–15a*
*Psalm 138*
*Matthew 7:7–12*

Prayer seems to be a neglected aspect of life for some modern Christians. This is unfortunate, because prayer is the way in which we acknowledge our dependency on God; that is why the Gospels show Jesus at prayer so often. Today we might take the lead from the readings and make this our prayer:

"Help me, Lord, for I am weak and powerless on my own. I am unable to treat others as I wish to be treated because of my sinfulness and human limitations. I am seeking your assistance; I am knocking and asking for the ability to live and to love as did Christ Your Son."

# FRIDAY

## WEEK I

*Ezekiel 18:21–28*
*Psalm 130*
*Matthew 5:20–26*

Jesus reminds us that our holiness must surpass that of the scribes and Pharisees. These people observed the Law, and many of them were very devout, but Jesus goes beyond the demands of law and strict justice—He wants love exhibited. "Thou shalt not kill" becomes "Love your enemies." "Thou shalt not commit adultery" becomes "Any man who looks lustfully at a woman commits adultery." The practice of Christianity, then, does not mean doing the minimum but the maximum; Jesus requires us to walk the "extra mile."

# SATURDAY

## WEEK I

*Deuteronomy 26:16–19*
*Psalm 119*
*Matthew 5:43–48*

Many Christians have a very individualistic approach to religion: *It's between me and God.* But it isn't. The Judaeo-Christian Tradition emphasizes the fact, as does today's First Reading, that we are called to be a holy people, a community of faith. Of course, individual effort is important, for that is how the community will be built up, but the individual Christian must be conscious of his community role and responsibility. The call to perfection is given to each person in the hope that each will respond. Thus, Jesus will be able to present to His Father a "people peculiarly His own."

# WEEK TWO OF LENT

# SECOND SUNDAY

## YEAR A

*Genesis 12:1–4a*
*Psalm 33*
*2 Timothy 1:8b–10*
*Matthew 17:1-9*

In the spring of 1980, I had the privilege of visiting the Holy Land for the first time—including the opportunity to celebrate Mass on Mount Tabor, the site of Our Lord's Transfiguration. It took us more than thirty minutes to scale that mountain—by car. Only after that day could I fully appreciate Peter's suggestion to Jesus that they build some tents and stay a while! After all, they had trekked up on foot. Seriously, though, what does the Transfiguration represent?

This strange event asks believers to look to another dimension of existence. Like Abram, we are urged to "go forth . . . to a land"—that God will show us. To apprehend the experience, one must be willing to view reality from the perspective of the unforeseeable future, rather than from the limited present.

So often, we hear people say: "If only I could have been there with Peter, James, and John, then my life in Christ would be so different, so much stronger." Ah, but you have been there—many times over. Each time we participate in the Church's liturgy, we transcend the constricting categories of space and time; we venture into eternity. As a result, we see Jesus in a new and different light, thus seeing ourselves transformed by the action of divine grace.

Consider these sacramental encounters as the continuation of the mystery of the Transfiguration. Baptism inserts one into the process and radically transforms that person into a new creation. Penance restores life to a soul dead through sin. The Eucharist is the means through which the Head and members of Christ's Church are wondrously united in a bond of intimacy and charity. I think you get the point.

Good liturgy does for us what the Transfiguration did for the Apostles—it allows us to face with trust—and even joy—the cross in our own lives, confident of final victory, a victory re-presented in each liturgical encounter.

Good liturgy, like the Transfiguration before it, impels us to "go forth" with the Word of the Risen Christ received in the Church, spreading His Gospel by a testimony given not only with our lips but with our very lives. In other words, the liturgy we celebrate on Mount Tabor renews us as witnesses in the world to the glory of the Transfigured Christ.

Good liturgy, in short, "makes manifest" the "grace held out to us in Christ Jesus before the world began." It gives us a glimpse of what awaits us in the life to come; it provides us with the incentive to push on to the finish line, where we will see God as He is—in the eternal liturgy of Heaven. The Church's liturgy, then, transports us to Mount Tabor—even if so briefly, helping us to behold the Transfigured Christ, in Whom we find ourselves transfigured.

# SECOND SUNDAY

## YEAR B

*Genesis 22:1–2, 9, 10–13, 15–18*
*Psalm 116*
*Romans 8:31b–34*
*Mark 9:2–10*

We are confronted today with an impressive scene in the Gospel: a mountain, dazzling garments, a cloud, divine majesty, a heavenly voice. Anyone familiar with the Old Testament will see a direct parallel to God's appearance to Moses on Mount Sinai when the Law was given. Today, however, the Law is not a list of rules, but a Person: "Listen to *Him*!"

Why should we listen to Him? Because this Person, like Isaac, is ready to lay down His life in obedience to the Father's will. In other words, He means what He says, and His life is concrete proof of that. Jesus does not ask us to do one thing as He does another. No, He makes great demands, but He Himself shows us how to meet those demands. In Jesus, we learn that God is on our side—that God loves us enough to provide us with the example of His own Son.

What is Jesus asking of us today? Very simply put, to be like Him. That means we must be obedient like Abraham and Jesus, concerned about fulfilling the Law and the Prophets symbolized by the presence of Moses and Elijah in today's scene. Christ's two-fold command of love of God and neighbor is the complete fulfillment of the Law and the Prophets; both loves are absolutely necessary and are, in fact, two sides of the same coin. God must be the top priority in my life, and any person or thing that takes me from that single goal is leading me into idolatry.

Then, that pure and unique love of God must be translated into action on behalf of other people. That's why Peter was wrong to suggest staying on the mountain in ecstasy. Yes, there are times when even prayer can be out of place. The experience of God on the mountain should have made the Apostles ready and willing to share that experience with others. The situation remains the same today. "I need prayer—I need action!" That is the message Jesus gives His Apostles in the Transfiguration. That is also the message of His own life, as He frequently paused from what must have been a hectic schedule to commune with His heavenly Father.

Each year the Season of Lent gives us the opportunity to withdraw for a short period of time to evaluate, to strengthen, to recommit, to renew, to regain perspective—and the Church hopes that our encounter with God in those more intense moments of communication will give us the wherewithal to leave the mountain and return to the task at hand of witnessing to the Gospel in the various circumstances of our lives.

Today we hear the Father encouraging the Apostles—and us—to listen to Jesus, Who is the fulfillment of the Law and the Prophets, and we recall, with gratitude, that we are part of that Covenant people begun by Abraham and redeemed by Christ. We also learn in the school of the Scriptures that obedience to God is always rewarded, and that He never tests us beyond our capabilities. Therefore, even though the commandment of listening to and following Jesus, the perfect Lover, is not easy, we believe the job can be done, because we have an ace in the hole for, as Paul reminds us: "If God is for us, who can be against us?"

# SECOND SUNDAY

## YEAR C

*Genesis 15:5–12, 17–18*
*Psalm 27*
*Philippians 3:17- 4:1*
*Luke 9:28–36*

Of all the events recorded in the New Testament, perhaps none has raised more questions or caused more confusion than the Transfiguration, which we hear about today. Of all the aspects of the Christian life, perhaps none is more misunderstood than prayer. What do these two seemingly unrelated situations have to do with each other? They are definitely related because both deal with having contact with God, encountering the presence of the Divine. If Lent could accomplish anything, it should help us deepen our prayer life; it should make our contacts with God more real and more frequent. Let's spend some time today thinking about prayer, using the Apostles' experience of the Transfiguration as a model.

Prayer is seeking reality. Some people, Christians included, have the notion that prayer is a way of escaping reality. Nothing could be further from the correct theology of prayer. Peter wanted to use prayer in that way, it seems, but Jesus did not allow that to happen. Peter had found the experience of the Divine to be a comforting thing, a nice feeling, and he didn't want to let go. However, the Apostles could not stay on the Mount of the

Transfiguration—there was work to be done in the world, and they had to do it. Good prayer provides us with encounters with God that should give us the strength that we need to get through times of doubt and confusion—it is never a substitute for reality. Surely Jesus intended the Transfiguration to be a means of helping His Apostles confront the harsh realities of His Passion and Death, yet to come.

Genuine prayer is a conversation. That means communication, which is never easy and which always requires real effort. It also implies that we are involved in a dialogue, a point most people neglect in prayer. We are usually quite good at telling God what we need, but we fail to allow Him to respond. The Father's advice was important: "This is my beloved Son—listen to Him." We dislike silence and listening, so we often fill in the gaps with our own answers, rather than waiting for His. Some years ago a second-grader was teasing one of his classmates about not getting the bike for Christmas for which he had prayed all during Advent. "You prayed and prayed, and God didn't answer your prayer," said the one fellow. "Yes, He did," the other responded, "He said, *No!*" That little guy knew the meaning of listening—he also knew another aspect of prayer that we need to consider.

He knew, at least subconsciously, that when we approach God in prayer, we must be willing to be changed by Him and to have our desires conformed to His Will. Jesus exemplified this most clearly in His final agony, during which He asked His Father for release, but ended

His prayer with an attitude of submission: "Yet not my will, but Thine be done."

We must also have a regular routine of prayer. It must be as natural a part of our lives as eating and breathing. Otherwise, we run the risk of falling into that trap of using God when we want Him and ignoring Him when we don't. That kind of prayer is not only cheap—it's immature. There are also very special times in life that require us to "get away from it all," moments when we have to be alone with God—in times of crisis or before important decisions—on a retreat, when we try to have a kind of "second honeymoon" with God. Today's Gospel story was one of those unique occasions.

The Apostles' initial reaction to beholding the glorified Christ was one of fear—and that is a very normal reaction. It can be terrifying to experience the Presence and Power of God, because we then realize the tremendous gap that exists between His holiness and ours. Nevertheless, we continue to deepen our relationship with the All-Holy God because that is the only way we will ever even come close to our ultimate goals of sharing in His holiness.

Peter, James, and John profited greatly from getting a glimpse of Christ in glory; it helped them understand the glory to which they were called. Prayer works in exactly the same way for us—it enables us to keep our gaze fixed on the finish line as we realize that the moments of happiness, known now in prayer, are but an obscure shadow of the joys yet to come.

# MONDAY

## WEEK II

*Daniel 9:4b–10*
*Psalm 79*
*Luke 6:36–38*

Sin is a part of human existence and, for that reason, will always be with us. The difficulty in our day is that very few people are able to accept this fact. Many make a habit of rationalizing, so that one psychiatrist could write a book entitled: "Whatever Became of Sin?"

If we can take a good honest look at ourselves and accept ourselves as sinners, then we have put ourselves on the road to perfection. Like David, the Christian admits: "I have sinned, I have done wrong." And he quickly adds, "But with Your help, I can be the kind of person You want me to be."

# TUESDAY

## WEEK II

*Isaiah 10:16–20*
*Psalm 50*
*Matthew 23:1–12*

The most Christian thing we can do is always to hope for a brighter future; in fact, that is God's constant promise: "Things will get better."

Christians believe that it is never too late to change the course of one's life—to return to the Lord, regardless of how many or how serious our past failings. Lent is the season for rekindling our hopes that God will show us His saving power. It is also the time to commit ourselves to an intensive self-searching of our actions and attitudes, realizing that even if our "sins be like scarlet, they may become white as snow."

# WEDNESDAY

## WEEK II

*Jeremiah 18:18–20*
*Psalm 31*
*Matthew 20:17–28*

Today we see Jesus resolutely setting His face toward Jerusalem, where He was to encounter suffering and death. Jesus not only taught us how to live—He also taught us how to die.

Death is the most inevitable and fearful part of life, and Jesus gives the perfect example. He shows that the best way to die is to live well. In this way, we do not shrink from death. Rather, we accept it with the confidence that we are drinking from the cup of Jesus, and in the hope that this cup which brings death also contains the "potion of immortality."

# THURSDAY

## WEEK II

*Jeremiah 17:5–10*
*Psalm 1*
*Luke 16:19–31*

Today's Gospel is not so much about Lazarus as it is about the behavior of the rich man. We all know people like him, who want the best of both worlds and stop at nothing to achieve their goals.

A very simple but profound lesson is at the heart of today's reading: Our heaven or hell is in the making right now. And, it is proportionate to the heaven or hell we are creating for the people with whom we live and work.

# FRIDAY

## WEEK II

*Genesis 37:3–4, 12–13a, 17b–28*
*Psalm 105*
*Matthew 21:33–43, 45–46*

Joseph and Jesus shared several common characteristics. Joseph angered his brothers because he was his father's fair-haired boy; Jesus roused the hostility of the religious authorities of His day because He dared to speak of the unique relationship He had with the Father and Creator of us all. Joseph annoyed his brothers with his dreams; Jesus was a stumbling-block because of His dream: That men could yield a rich harvest—indeed had to do so—under the influence of divine grace.

Jesus went on to assert that those who cooperate with God's grace could share in His special relationship with the Father. This was the "Impossible Dream" for many. Therefore, He was dismissed as a "nut" or a "blasphemer" by them. They rejected Him and sold Him for thirty pieces of silver. But the Scriptures go on to say that ". . . to those who accepted Him, He gave the power to become the children of God." That is His promise, and that is our hope.

# SATURDAY

## WEEK II

*Micah 7:14–15, 18–20*
*Psalm 103*
*Luke 15:1–3, 11–32*

In the Gospel reading we see a boy who was dead but who came back to life. Dead, because he left his father and his home. Alive, because he returned. Lent is a time for us to make our passage from death to life. Although the Prodigal Son's motives for returning home were not the best, at least he knew how good home was, and he still remembered how to go back. Let us pray that today God will move at least one sinner to come back home.

# WEEK THREE OF LENT

# THIRD SUNDAY

## YEAR A

*Exodus 17:3–7*
*Psalm 95*
*Romans 5:1–2, 5–8*
*John 4:5–42*

John's Gospel is shot through with examples of irony and misunderstanding. In fact, much of the agenda is moved along by the very dullness and thick-headedness of so many of the characters. The first century's answer to Zsa Zsa Gabor, whom we meet in today's reading, is a case in point. Her encounter with Jesus could well be accompanied by the show-tune "Getting to Know You."

The focus of this episode, you see, is not so much on her adulterous background but on Jesus' identity; who she is/was is nothing compared to Who He is, for Who He is will transform her into who she will be. The Samaritan woman undergoes a growth in understanding. At the outset, she regards Jesus as an ordinary man. Gradually, she comes to view Him as a prophet and then as the Messiah. Finally, He is acclaimed the "Savior of the world." In that process, His identity affects hers—and ours.

This passage is also a reflection on the grace of *Election*—what it means to be chosen. In the divine-human relationship, God always takes the initiative. Hence,

Jesus approaches her, with no regard for her ethnicity or sex or pattern of behavior—in violation of all the rules of Jewish law and etiquette.

Initially, we find a woman fixated on the physical—and not any too bright, either: "You have no bucket; I get tired of making too many trips to the well; this must be a good place to worship because my ancestors did it here." Jesus, perhaps with some inner amusement, takes her as she is and elevates her mind so that she can look beyond the apparent and the immediate—to the possibility of receiving "living water." In fact, John tells us that even the disciples still had some distance to go to adopt a genuinely supernatural orientation. The change occurs because Jesus patiently moves her, and them, and us in that direction.

What was the result? The adulteress became an evangelist, we learn. How? She allowed herself to be touched by One Who had reached out to her. Was He a prophet? The Messiah? Yes, and more, the very "Savior of the world!" What Jesus did for the Samaritan woman was not an offering for a special one-day sale. It is part of His on-going program as our "fountain of life-giving waters" and our "food"—in Baptism and the Eucharist. They, of course, are the reasons for Paul's hymn to hope, for they are the means by which we are justified, or put right with God.

So, what is your particular sin? Adultery? Fornication? Hatred? Revenge? Artificial contraception? Whatever it is, remember: "It is precisely in this that God proves His love for us: That while we were still sinners,

Christ died for us." Yes, Christ did die for us; now He wants us to live for Him. Will you accept the Savior's invitation to drink from the "fountain of eternal life"? The Samaritan woman did and thus discovered important things about Him and about herself. You could do the same, "if you only *recognized* God's gift."

# THIRD SUNDAY

## YEAR B

*Exodus 20:1–17*
*Psalm 19*
*1 Corinthians 1:22–25*
*John 2:13–25*

We have just come through a period in the Church's history when many, including clergy and theologians, had begun to question the relevance of the Ten Commandments. They're so negative, so restrictive of freedom, so tending toward the subservient. But the real thinkers and scholars have always tried to view the Commandments as the ancient Hebrews did—in a most positive light.

What accounts for the difference in attitude between the Hebrews and so many of us? The Hebrews were absolutely convinced that God cared for them. They recalled His creative activity at the dawn of time, His liberation of them from bondage, and His formation of the Israelite nation. They realized, in ways we frequently forget, that they were a Chosen People who had a unique relationship with the Lord. Because of their covenant, they had been called to give visible, public witness to their election for all the nations to see.

In return for the special love they had received, the Hebrews were to observe the Lord's Commandments. They never balked, because they trusted in God's on-going love and mercy, a mercy for which they had already witnessed more than ample proof. In reality, they were being asked to do very little—to trust a loving Father and to believe that He had a better idea regarding what would bring the greatest measure of happiness to both individual and community.

In our romantic idealism and liberalism, we moderns have often thought that law is a stumbling block to human growth and development, but that need not be so and usually is not so. Rules and regulations can often provide for the best conditions under which individuals can truly blossom as persons. Law can be a very liberating kind of thing because it protects me from oppression by others and from oppression by some of my own base instincts, which I might sooner deny.

A rabbi recounted the story of how annoying and inhibiting traffic lights once seemed to him. He was sure that the twenty-minute trip from his home to his synagogue could be cut in half without the lights. One day there was a power outage, and there were no lights. The twenty-minute trip took two hours because of the massive confusion that resulted. He discovered, the hard way, that the short-term annoyance brought him to his destination more quickly and more safely.

And that is precisely how we should view the Ten Commandments—as vehicles that inform us of God's will and facilitate our arrival home by the safest, surest, and swiftest way possible. Undoubtedly, these were the thoughts in the mind of the Psalmist as he sang, "The law of the Lord is perfect, refreshing the soul."

The Church gives us Lent as an annual season of covenant renewal—an opportunity to deepen our relationship with the God Who called the Hebrews of old and us today to be a holy people. And while a popular song tells us that "all you need is love," an equally popular line reminds us that "actions speak louder than words." Today's Gospel reading informed us that Jesus "was aware of what was in man's heart." If we claim to have the love of God in our hearts, we need to show forth that love by an enthusiastic and grateful living of God's blueprint for our happiness. Because God does know best and because He loves us so much, He gave us this code to live by—as Commandments, not suggestions. The only wise response is loving obedience.

# THIRD SUNDAY

## YEAR C

*Exodus 3:1–8a, 13–15*
*Psalm 103*
*1 Corinthians 10:1–6, 10–12*
*Luke 13:1–9*

God gives us the season of Lent to become saints; in fact, God gives us our whole life to be saints. God is also patient as we work on becoming saints, giving us plenty of time, but today's Gospel reminds us that God does call for a final reckoning. He expects to see results.

What is the difference between a saint and a sinner? A saint sees himself as a sinner; he realizes, with St. Paul, that "all men have sinned and fall short of the glory of God." A saint realizes with St. Paul that "anyone who thinks he is standing upright" must "watch out lest he fall!" The sinner, on the other hand, sees himself as better than others, or at least not as bad as others. The sinner ultimately offends either through presumption ("God will understand") or through despair ("My sins are too great to be forgiven").

Does God expect the impossible, that within forty days our personality will be completely overhauled? No, but He does expect progress. Our life in Christ can never be a stagnant affair. If we are not moving forward toward our goal, we are falling behind. The Church's hope is that if we use this forty-day period to die to all those things (or at least some of those things) that keep us from growing closer to Jesus, we shall indeed experience a new life with our Risen Lord on Easter Sunday. Lent, however, is not just a preparation for Easter; it is a preparation for eternity—an everlasting Easter given to all who have been baptized into Christ's Death and Resurrection, have partaken of that spiritual food we call the Eucharist, and have modeled their lives on those faithful men and women we honor as saints.

Sanctity is not being a plaster statue with a pious appearance. Sanctity is a state of being comfortable in the presence of God. It does not consist in making a big splash; it comes much nearer to St. Thérèse's idea of the "little way" by which we do the ordinary things extraordinarily well. In fact, all the saints would concur: "It is trifles that make perfection, but perfection is no trifle."

How do people become saints? They are not surprised on the day they face Christ in judgment or on the day of their canonization. They work on becoming saints their whole life long as they cooperate with God's grace. Their success gives us reason to hope that we, too, can share in the experience of blessedness. God does not keep sanctity for the few; He offers it to all.

Yes, God is good: He gives us Lent; He gives us life itself; He gives us saints—all that we might become saints ourselves. "All you saints of God, *pray for us that we may be made worthy of the promises of Christ.*"

# MONDAY

## WEEK III

*2 Kings 5:1–15a*
*Psalm 42*
*Luke 4:24–30*

Judaism at the time of Jesus became very exclusive, and Jesus reminds them that this is not God's plan. Many Catholics also have the opinion that Catholicism is like belonging to the "in-group" or God's "jet set," but God has no such idea. God is for all men, and thank God for that. Why? Because that means He is for you.

# TUESDAY

## WEEK III

*Daniel 3:2, 11–20*
*Psalm 25*
*Matthew 18:21–35*

Today's First Reading seems so appropriate for the modern Church. We often seem to be just floating, without leaders and without direction, especially in some dioceses. But we are trying to please God and are trying to live up to the ideals of Jesus.

Maybe this prayer of the great twentieth-century monk Thomas Merton could be ours; in part, it reads: ". . . Nor do I really know myself, and the fact that I think I am following Your will does not mean that I am actually doing so. But I believe that the desire to please You does in fact please You, and I hope that I have that desire in all that I am doing."

# WEDNESDAY

## WEEK III

*Deuteronomy 4:1, 5–9*
*Psalm 147*
*Matthew 5:17–19*

Commandments are not very popular today. We are told that love is all that matters; understood correctly, that is quite true. Today Jesus suggests that His followers should keep God's laws. Why? Because obedience is a sign of love—we obey to the degree that we love. Perhaps we could spend this day concentrating on one particular aspect of our life that needs improvement. Work on it today in response to Jesus' invitation to fulfill the Law and to become perfect like our Father in Heaven. For then we shall be called "great in the kingdom of God."

# THURSDAY

## WEEK III

*Jeremiah 7:23–28*
*Psalm 95*
*Luke 11:14–23*

More than a century ago, Abraham Lincoln delivered his famous "House Divided" speech, for which he obtained his inspiration from this Gospel passage.

Our nation is once again a "house divided," as it is pulled in two directions by opposing forces. The advocates of abortion, divorce, pornography, and sexual license call for their lifestyle to be given "equal time" with the way of life that has its roots in the origin of our country, indeed, in the Judaeo-Christian Tradition itself. The task of every committed Christian is to be a voice for God in society, just like the Prophets of old.

That means we must know God's Word, live its message in our own lives, and then invite others to do the same. It is the work of a lifetime, but Lent is a good time to start, lest our land continue to be a "House Divided," instead of "one nation under God."

# FRIDAY

## WEEK III

*Hosea 14:1-9*
*Psalm 81*
*Mark 12:28b–34*

Some people have the mistaken notion that love was absent from the Old Testament. In today's Gospel, we see how wrong such a theory is. With our Jewish friends, we are called to worship one God, to love Him above all else, and to love others because of Him. This is not easy. It calls for single-minded perseverance and a deep commitment to religious values. But for us in the Judaeo-Christian Tradition, it is the only way to attain salvation—because that is God's way. And, one who follows His way is "not far from the reign of God."

# SATURDAY

## WEEK III

*Hosea 5:15c–6:6*
*Psalm 51*
*Luke 18:9–14*

So often Catholics have been accused of empty externalism, and sometimes the charges are well founded. Today
we hear Hosea say that God is not interested in religious
rites unless we put our faith into practice.

Many have been making an added effort to participate in the Eucharist during Lent, and that is surely
praiseworthy. But, that effort must be matched by a
similar eagerness to bring the Gospel into our homes
and places of business. Otherwise, what we do at Mass
loses its meaning, for we become Pharisees who are
more concerned with looking good than with being
good.

# WEEK FOUR OF LENT

# FOURTH SUNDAY

## YEAR A

*1 Samuel 16:1b, 6–7, 10–13a*
*Psalm 23*
*Ephesians 5:8–14*
*John 9:1–41*

Have you ever lost your sight—even temporarily? Have you ever been plunged into darkness unexpectedly? It is frightening and fearsome. "Darkness/light; night/day, and blindness/sight" are themes frequently repeated in John because he wanted to teach some important truths about Jesus and the nature of Christianity through these familiar human experiences of reality.

In today's Gospel we see a study in contrast presented for our consideration. We meet the man born blind, through no fault of his own; he is eager to see both spiritually and physically—he is open to the workings of God. Then we encounter a group of Pharisees, who have physical sight but have become spiritually blinded because they have lost all perspective—instead of rejoicing in the healing of the blind man, they react to the fact that Jesus has healed on the Sabbath. These men prove true the adage that says: "There are none so blind as those who will not see." What John has done, then, is to present us with examples of two types of people we always have with us: People who are willing to accept Jesus as the "Light of the World" and people who are unwilling to do so.

As Christians, we claim to be followers of Jesus, the "Light of the World." St. Paul repeatedly admonished his disciples to "walk honorably as in the daylight." But how do you know if you are doing so?

An old rabbi once asked his students how to tell when the long night is over and the new day has begun. One student suggested: "Is it when you can see through the shadows at fifty yards and tell the difference between a dog and a sheep?" " No," replied the rabbi. Another ventured: "Is it when you can tell at a great distance the difference between a fig tree and a peach tree?" The rabbi shook his head in disagreement. Finally, the students said: " If you are so wise, you tell us." The rabbi paused for a moment and then said: "It is when you can look on the face of any woman or man and see a sister, a brother. If you cannot do that, then no matter what time it is, it is still night."

On this Fourth Sunday in Lent, Jesus, the "Light of the World," is asking you: What time of day is it in your life?

# FOURTH SUNDAY

## YEAR B

*2 Chronicles 36:14–16, 19–23*
*Psalm 137*
*Ephesians 2:4–10*
*John 3:14–21*

Christianity is an on-going exchange of gifts between God and man. As in all things, God took the initiative and gave such a fantastic Gift that all of ours offered in return tend to pale into insignificance. John reminds us of that event when he says: "God so loved the world that He gave His only Son, that whoever believes in Him may not die but may have eternal life."

Throughout salvation history, God has been known as a generous Person. He created the universe with a sense of abandon and lavishness that few of us would even consider duplicating, if we could. He fashioned the nomadic Hebrews into a mighty nation and then gave them the Law on Mount Sinai to help them maintain their relationship with Him. But in the fullness of time, God gave the deepest sign and most profound proof of His unending love by giving us the wonderful gift of His Son.

God's actions give us a hint as to His expectations of us. Our gracious and loving Father has given us an example. His example is not designed to condemn us but to save us. St. Paul tells us that our response to God's kindness to us should be a life of good deeds. In other words, we must return to God, and to other people, with the same degree of generosity the favors we have so readily received.

Lent is a time to stress many of the really important matters in our living of the Christian life. One of those is charity. I hate to talk about money from the pulpit because the Church is so often accused of being overly concerned about finances, yet I also realize that from time to time I have an obligation to remind the faithful of their obligation to be a giving people. Every Christian needs to be charitable as a sign of gratitude for God's goodness to him and as a way of concretely supporting the works of charity and the advancement of religion. This is not just a nice idea—it is an absolute necessity, flowing from our baptismal commitment to be mission-minded and other-directed.

A Christian's first obligation is to his family—to see to it that all the necessities of life are provided for. Next in importance is an enthusiastic support of one's parish by work and donations. Finally, the Christian must be involved, to the degree that it is financially possible, in the worldwide mission of the Church, so that others may come to know about this God Who has loved us enough to give us His very own Son.

A story is told about a tavern found among the ruins of Pompeii. On the walls of that establishment, the owner jotted down the credit extended to customers. When Vesuvius erupted without warning, all debts had been paid, except for one. The lava froze that city into a state of permanence at that very point in time—and there it remains today.

All of us have debts we owe to God and our fellow man, and we must not pass up a single opportunity to pay these debts while we can and whenever we can. Otherwise, we run the risk of leaving this world with unfulfilled obligations and debts that stand against us forever.

# FOURTH SUNDAY

## YEAR C

*Joshua 5:9, 10–12*
*Psalm 34*
*2 Corinthians 5:17–21*
*Luke 15:1–3, 11–32*

Today's parable of the prodigal son is a story that is familiar to us all from childhood, and yet one so rich in meaning that it can never be fully exploited. An angle on it that I thought might be interesting to consider today was what this parable has to say about a very contemporary problem—materialism. Both sons in the story were deeply attached to the good things in life; the "hero", however, was so enamored of them that he wanted them all—immediately. That caused his problem to begin with. His return home was equally motivated by materialism; he wanted to come home only when he had run out of money abroad. What does all this have to do with us?

When the history of our era is written, it may well be referred to as the "Age of Materialism." Materialism is characterized by a desire for immediate self-gratification of physical wants, a grasping greediness, a willingness to gain more at the expense of those who have less, an immature attitude more concerned with receiving than with giving. One need only look at the advertising media to see how true this is. They know how modern people think and act, and they appeal to those baser instincts for their own benefit.

Don't get me wrong—material things are not bad, if for no other reason than that they were created by God. However, they can become bad when they lead us away from God and other people, rather than bringing us into a closer union with the Christ Who was poor and so loves the poor today. Lent is a time given to us to balance out our excessive materialism, as we do without things to deepen a relationship with a Person. Almsgiving is a traditional Lenten practice by which we give to those in need—not simply from our surplus but from our substance. Mother Teresa used to say, "You know you are giving sacrificially and from the heart if your giving hurts."

Most of us have never known hunger or homelessness. For that reason we need to ponder the words of Pope John Paul II that he spoke at the Yankee Stadium Mass in 1979. Let his words on wealth and concern for the poor guide your conduct in how you react to appeals of charity. On that occasion he spoke about the rich man and Lazarus: "Was the rich man condemned because he had riches, because he abounded in earthly possessions, because he 'dressed in purple linen and feasted splendidly every day'? No, I would say that it was not for this reason. The rich man was condemned because he did not pay attention to the other man. Nowhere does Christ condemn the mere possession of earthly goods as such. Instead, He pronounces very harsh words against those who use their possessions in a selfish way—without paying attention to the needs of others. The parable of the rich man and Lazarus must always be present in our memory; it must form our conscience."

The heresy of materialism makes a tragic mistake: it substitutes the worship of the creature for that of the Creator. I recently came upon a poem that says that people who have fallen prey to that philosophy of life are in for a rude awakening at the end of time:

I had been dead but a few minutes.
I felt myself soaring into the heavens.
I approached the Holy of Holies
With heart-pounding excitement.
How magnificent it will be!
(For the gods have everything.)
I recalled the old stories: thrilling harps,
Gates of pearl, pavements of gold, graceful angels.
I imagined the dazzling beauty, the luxurious
    furnishings.
The splendid decor, the delicious feasts.
I entered.
There was nothing.
I repeat, nothing!
Then it dawned on me.
Of course!
To be holy is to need nothing.

# MONDAY

## WEEK IV

*Isaiah 65:17–21*
*Psalm 30*
*John 4:43–54*

The Jesus we meet in John's Gospel works several signs—in fact, His signs are His "calling card"—they tell us Who He is and what He is about. A recurrent theme is that "seeing leads to believing."

During Lent we are given the opportunity to become more faithful signs of Christ alive today—by our fidelity to the Gospel; by our sensitivity to people in need. Let us hope people will see us in action and so come to faith.

# TUESDAY

## WEEK IV

*Ezekiel 47:1-9, 12*
*Psalm 46*
*John 5:1–16*

Lent began as a preparation period for converts to Christianity. Therefore, one of the topics under consideration is Baptism, which today's readings bring to mind.

Water is an element of power—for good and evil. It can give life to beautiful flowers, or it can destroy whole cities. The waters through which the Hebrews passed safely were the very waters that crushed the power of the Egyptians. The waters of Baptism bring death to sin but life in God. Are these waters bringing us life and salvation, or are they closing in like a menacing flood? It depends on our cooperation with God's original plan and offer of salvation.

# WEDNESDAY

## WEEK IV

*Isaiah 49:8–15*
*Psalm 145*
*John 5:17–30*

Jesus makes resurrection dependent on hearing the voice of God—an interesting and very logical connection. In other words, only those will be able to rise to glorious eternal life who have consistently heeded God's voice as it came to them in His Commandments, for they will be used to His voice; they will know its sound. This is quite a consolation for those who take God's Word seriously. But to those who listen or act half-heartedly, God gives this season to sharpen our hearing, so that we may hear God's voice on the last day and live forever.

# THURSDAY

## WEEK IV

*Exodus 32:7–14*
*Psalm 106*
*John 5:31–47*

Jesus makes a crushing statement to His audience today: "You do not have the love of God in your hearts!" What motivated Him to say such a thing? Their rejection of His message; their preconceived notions; their hypocrisy—their lack of charity. How many so-called "good Christians" have the same flaws? Let us work at replacing these attitudes with an openness to God's Word, so that Jesus will never have to say that we are not possessed of the love of God.

# FRIDAY

## WEEK IV

*Wisdom 2:1a, 12–22*
*Psalm 34*
*John 7:1–2, 10, 25–30*

In John's Gospel we hear a great deal about Jesus' "hour of glory." What is it? When did it occur? Most of us would suggest the Resurrection, but not John. No, Jesus' "hour of glory" begins with His Passion. Why? Because Jesus was never more a King than when He bravely and willingly accepted His Father's plan for Him. And therein lies the lesson for us. We do not have to wait for the end of time for our "hour of glory." No, it begins when we accept God's plan for us, including suffering and death. By accepting them, we master them and so begin our "hour of glory." Because of Christ, suffering and death have meaning; because of our attitude, resurrection is not a complete surprise but the next logical step.

# SATURDAY

## WEEK IV

*Jeremiah 11:18–20*
*Psalm 7*
*John 7:40–53*

A Christian is a person who has entrusted his cause to God, after the example of Jesus. A Christian is one who believes and hopes and loves, in spite of adversity. A Christian is a person who can be put down for a time but one who inevitably rises again. And all of this is so because of the firm conviction expressed by St. Paul: "For those who love God, all things work together for the good."

# WEEK FIVE OF LENT

# FIFTH SUNDAY

## YEAR A

*Ezekiel 37:12–14*
*Psalm 130*
*Romans 8:8–11*
*John 11:1–45*

We have heard a lot over the years about people who have supposedly experienced death and have, somehow or other, come back to life. Today we meet one such gentleman in the gospel—Lazarus. What is the point of reading this Gospel on this particular Sunday?

First of all, John constructed his Gospel in such a way that we encounter Jesus working six signs, each one building in importance until we reach the sixth and greatest—the raising of Lazarus from the dead. John wanted to show the connection between the work of Jesus and the work of God at the dawn of Creation, for Jesus was bringing about a "New Creation." John also used this Lazarus episode as a kind of sneak preview of Jesus' own Resurrection. But I think the Church wants us to consider Lazarus in the tomb and to ask ourselves if we are not in some way like him.

Each of us lives in his own private tomb so often. Like Lazarus, we are bound head and foot by our faults and sins, which keep us from living full Christian lives. Am I a racist? Am I unconcerned about the welfare of others? Am I addicted to alcohol, or gambling, or sex, or drugs?

Am I mastered by the spirit of materialism abroad in the world today? If so, I am among the living dead, and today, Jesus summons me to come forth from the tomb of my personal sinfulness with all the force He used in raising Lazarus, as He says: "Peter, Anne, Mary, Joe . . . Come out!"

How can I share in this Lazarus experience? By opening myself to the Word of God, by a change of heart, by using this Lenten season as a time of self-examination and growth, by adopting a new course and direction in my life, and by returning to the Lord and the community of the Church through the Sacrament of Penance. Jesus wants us all to be a part of His "New Creation," but belief in Jesus and lives of sin are incompatible, so we must heed the Lord's call to follow Him and make Him the focus of our lives and our love. Jesus is just as eager to do for us what He did for Lazarus, and we will hear Him say those same powerful and comforting words: "Untie him and let him go free!"

# FIFTH SUNDAY

## YEAR B

*Jeremiah 31:31–34*
*Psalm 51*
*Hebrews 5:7–9*
*John 12:20–33*

Did you ever notice that there is a power in weakness? Consider the ability of a helpless child to elicit sympathy and assistance. Or, how often has an invalid been able to touch the hardest of hearts? It is even accurate to maintain that there are some people who are more effective in death than they ever were in life. Surely, that is the case with Jesus.

By His Death, Jesus initiated that new covenant spoken of by Jeremiah, a covenant written on men's hearts. By His Death, Jesus was able to take His place at the Father's right hand, where He continually intercedes for us. By His Death, Jesus gave us all an example of absolute and final obedience to the Father's Will.

The lesson of the Cross, put in the simple and homey terms of a grain of wheat, teaches us that death can be simply the beginning of a bigger and better way of life. The lesson of the Cross lies in the understanding that obedience and total love yield a rich harvest. The lesson of the Cross strikes us to the core with the absurdity and the depravity of sin. The lesson of the Cross is a painful reminder of man's inhumanity to man—not only on a hill outside Jerusalem but in so many places and moments before and since. The lesson of the Cross gives us the most eloquent sermon possible on the depths of God's love for us.

Jesus knew that His effectiveness would grow because of His death and so He remarked: "And I . . . once I am lifted up from earth . . . will draw all men to Myself." Yes, Jesus, like a magnet, draws people to Himself—not through grandiose displays of power but by the humble and loving testimony given in His moment of greatest weakness—on the Cross. However, it is important to recall that His hour of suffering is likewise His hour of glory, for Jesus triumphed through His suffering.

In this drawing process, which Jesus exercises now, He invites us to join Him in His sufferings. He gave the very same invitation to His disciples. It was harder for them because they did not know the end of the story, and they had solid reasons for hesitance. We, however, know that our sufferings are united to His and that He took each and every one of them and offered them to the Father with His own. We also know, unlike the Apostles, how the story ends.

What is our excuse, then, for not following in the footsteps of Jesus, the "Suffering Servant"? Is it fear? Is it a lack of faith? Is it an unwillingness to die to those sinful attachments that really do need to die in our lives? In the remaining two weeks of Lent, I must look at my life more closely and very bluntly ask myself, "Why am I resisting the pull of the Crucified Lord?"

# FIFTH SUNDAY

## YEAR C

*Isaiah 43:16–21*
*Psalm 126*
*Philippians 3:8–14*
*John 8:1–11*

"On the breast of her gown, in red cloth . . . appeared the letter A." With that intriguing line, Nathaniel Hawthorne begins *The Scarlet Letter*, his story of a woman publicly branded as an adulteress. Some people would see in today's Gospel passage the directly opposite approach taken by Jesus. While I am not sure "opposite" is the right word, I would say it was very different. For a few minutes, let's explore Jesus' handling of the adulteress. For His style there is a pattern He used with every other kind of sinner—which obviously includes the way He relates Himself to you and me.

We usually speak of this woman as having been "caught in adultery." In reality, she was "caught" in more ways than one; she was caught between a vengeful crowd and a great Teacher, Whom she would only gradually come to know as a merciful Lord. Rather than look at her—as the crowd was intent on doing—let us fix our gaze on Jesus. What lessons can we learn?

First of all, we discover our Lord did not whitewash her behavior. He didn't blame an unloving mother or a bad neighborhood or a deprived childhood for her action. He didn't rationalize or psychologize her immorality or guilt away; He called "a spade a spade": "Avoid this *sin*," He commanded. Observe, too, that she never defended herself or made any excuses, either.

Secondly, we notice that Christ never defended her to the crowd. What He did do, however, was to place *her* sin in a broader context—namely, against the background of *their* sins. Thus were they all put in the untenable position of having to declare themselves sinless to qualify as potential condemners of her.

Thirdly, we find Jesus giving the adulteress—and us—the assurance that He is not out to harm anyone, let alone condemn. Being committed to the truth, though, He must remind her of the inappropriateness of her actions in the light of God's Law. The truth may not always be pleasant but, in the final analysis, it is liberating. After all, mercy means nothing if there is no reason to expect or hope for mercy. Mercy makes sense only if justice calls for condemnation.

We spend our whole lives long trying to balance the demands of justice with the demands of mercy; they seem so irreconcilable in our normal human experience—as parents, teachers, clergy, or just plain human beings. In God, however, justice and mercy are in perfect equilibrium. Believe it or not, we see it clearly operative in as unpleasant a subject as Hell. How so?

Who is God? St. John says, "God is love." What is sin? It is a refusal of love or a refusal to love. What is Heaven? It is possessing and being possessed by love for all eternity. On the final day, as the Lord judges our actions—

or, better yet, our lives-we must not appear as people who have consistently rejected love through sin, for God's justice will declare it so and then His mercy will allow us to choose our own deficient brand of happiness in an eternal Hell. God, you see, in His mercy will not force His love on us. And so, justice and mercy meet—just as they did for the woman caught in adultery.

Presumably, that woman took seriously Our Lord's advice (or command, really) about "sinning no more" because she was moved by His justice and mercy alike. What should be our response to this story? First, a prayer of thanksgiving to Almighty God for the many manifestations of His goodness to us. Second, a prayer of petition that, seeing ourselves as sinners, we would be as ready to extend mercy to others as we are to receive it for ourselves.

With whom did you most identify as you read today's Gospel? The woman? The crowd? Jesus? Your honest answer will tell you how near or far you are from the experience of salvation, which embraces both God's justice and God's mercy.

# MONDAY

## WEEK V

*Daniel 13:1–9, 15–17, 19–30, 33–62*
*Psalm 23*
*John 8:1–11*

Susanna stands in line with so many innocent people who are unjustly accused of wrong-doing: Mary, Jesus, Christians throughout the ages. This has happened to all of us at some time in our lives, and the best approach still remains Susanna's: Put the matter in God's hands.

On the other hand, the Gospel shows us people eager to judge and persecute; these have always been the hypocrites, not the righteous. The saint is so conscious of his failings that he would not dare judge others. May God grant each of us the insight to see ourselves as sinners, so that we can truly become saints.

# TUESDAY

## WEEK V

*Numbers 21:4–9*
*Psalm 102*
*John 8:21–30*

Jews hearing Jesus say "I am" so often were surely reminded of the sacred name, "Yahweh"—"I AM WHO AM." Today, Jesus says that we "will die in our sins" unless we accept Him. This is the uniqueness of Christianity: That it is not the following of a set of rules but the acceptance of a Person, a Person Who speaks for and is identified with God. Therefore, we are involved in a relationship, not a contract. Our sins do not break the "contract" as much as they hurt the One we claim to love, and so, Jesus presents Himself as the source of our salvation; by loving Him and following Him, we please the Father Who sent Him. This is the promise of Jesus; this is the Christian Faith: this is the basis for our fondest hopes.

# WEDNESDAY

## WEEK V

*Daniel 3:14–20, 91–92, 95*
*Daniel 3*
*John 8:31–42*

"The truth will set you free." This is one of the best-known verses of the New Testament but also rather perplexing because, in a few days, we will hear Pilate ask a question for all who ever come after him: "What is truth?"

Christians are not in search of truth, for if we follow Jesus, we have the "Truth." Yes, Jesus is the Truth Who sets us free. Jesus is the Liberator Who frees us from sin and self-seeking. He liberates us for life and love by offering the example of His life and teaching. If you are enslaved, come to Jesus, for "if the Son frees you, you will really be free."

# THURSDAY

## WEEK V

*Genesis 17:3–9*
*Psalm 105*
*John 8:51–59*

Very often people in the Scriptures received a new name when given a new mission; Abraham and Peter come to mind immediately. We, too, were given a new name—in Baptism—and the name is "Christian." And that name imposes obligations on us. It calls us to live as a covenant people—men and women who are especially and closely related to God through Christ. Our name requires us to be able to echo the words Jesus spoke about the Father: "Yes, I know Him well, and I keep His Word."

# FRIDAY

## WEEK V

*Jeremiah 20:10–13*
*Psalm 18*
*John 10:31–42*

Today Jesus quotes an Old Testament verse: "You are gods." Yes, that is our vocation. In every Mass, it is also our prayer: "May we come to share the divinity of Christ, Who humbled Himself to share our humanity." Our goal, then, is to be god-like. In the Old Testament, this seemed like an impossible dream, but, with the coming of Jesus, it is not only a promise but a firm reality. Each time we consciously choose God's way over our own, each time we exhibit sacrificial love, each time we share in this Eucharist and take Christ to ourselves, we are becoming more and more divine. For Christians, life is not a humanization process as much as it is a divinization process.

# SATURDAY

## WEEK V

*Ezekiel 37:21–28*
*Jeremiah 31*
*John 11:45–57*

Today, we see Caiaphas beginning the unfolding of the drama: He calls for Jesus to be a Victim. Christians, too, are called to be victims—not for themselves or their own salvation, but for the world. Our life-style should attract the interest and curiosity of the world, just as the life-style of Jesus did. The way we bear our sufferings and share our joys should bring the world to faith, and thus we will be continuing the work of Jesus "to gather into one all the dispersed children of God."

# HOLY WEEK

On Palm Sunday, the Church invites us to assume our roles in the drama of salvation, literally. The pagan philosopher Aristotle once observed that drama was the highest form of art because it enabled otherwise passive spectators to become active participants through the process of catharsis. Today we identify with the sinful crowd crying out for the death of the Lord of Life. Today we, far more importantly, empathize with the suffering Lord as we realize how human depravity was able to elicit the very depths of divine love.

The great French thinker Blaise Pascal declared that he would never entrust his life to any God Who was not willing to die for His people. This week assures us that we have just such a God in Christ.

# PALM SUNDAY

## YEAR A

*Isaiah 50:4–7*
*Psalm 22*
*Philippians 2:6–11*
*Matthew 26:14–27:66*

Thousands upon thousands come out today to greet Jesus as He rides into Jerusalem upon a donkey. At least, that is what we are trained to think was the case, having been brought up on Cecil B. DeMille-type productions, which foster such impressions. Of course, the Gospelwriters do provide DeMille with a basis for such an image. Let me raise a question, however, one not often raised: What would have happened had our blessed Lord entered Jerusalem in some other way? Would a cast of thousands still have welcomed Him? Might it have been different?

As a matter of fact, He did have another option. In traditional Jewish categories, Jesus had two modes of transportation at His disposal—both of which could have given clear signals about the nature of His mission, as He viewed it. The first possibility was for Jesus to mount a white steed; this would have said that He was Himself, as the conquering hero, destined to remove from Israel the yoke of Roman oppression. The second choice was the lowly donkey, which symbolized a Messiah in the mold of Isaiah's Suffering Servant, who regarded his role as essentially spiritual, redeeming Israel—and the whole world—not from the horrendous domination of Rome but from the far worse oppression of the Devil. And that is the signal that the Father's Son chose to send out on that first Palm Sunday.

If thousands did cheer His entry into Jerusalem, clearly understanding the message He was communicating, one can legitimately ask how many more would have turned out had they heard He had arrived on a white charger. However, the Savior did not worry about numbers at any time in His public life and ministry. Remember how He refused to modify His teaching on divorce and remarriage when the disciples expressed shock and dismay? Recall how He actually invited would-be followers to leave when they found His doctrine of the Eucharist too much to bear? No, Jesus was concerned with Truth, not popularity.

Interestingly enough, though, thousands did accept the message He proclaimed from His donkey; they were willing to follow a Suffering Servant, certainly aware of the fact that this called them to a similar fate. The Truth does have a strange attraction, and that is why they were compelled to shout from the housetops, literally, the ancient Hebrew acclamation that we have taken over into our celebration of the Eucharistic Sacrifice: *Benedictus qui venit in nomine Domini. Hosanna in excelsis.* They knew, deep down, that Jesus and His Word for them did indeed come from God, and that the only possible human and faith-filled response is the praise of God in the highest.

Throughout salvation history, Almighty God has never

been known to take the easy way in anything because He knows, in ways grasped only in shadowy form by us, that sacrifice reveals love in the most profound manner. Nor is God concerned with shallow display. If that were the case, He never would have come as a Babe at Bethlehem; He never would have come into Jerusalem astride a beast of burden; and He never would have come to us under the even more humble and unassuming forms of bread and wine in each renewal of His saving Death and Resurrection in the Mass.

Today's celebration calls us to make an act of faith in a God Who delights in challenging His people to a life of faith by offering them apparently simple signs to convey great depth of meaning. In but a few minutes we shall arrive at another one of the God-Man's entries into our world; like His entrance into Jerusalem nearly two thousand years ago, it signals sacrifice and death. With the eyes of faith, however, we see these otherwise depressing realities translated into the promise of eternal life, just as the elements of bread and wine are transformed into His very Body and Blood. And that is why it is so right to join our voices to those of the crowds of the ancient Hebrews; thus do we agree that God can indeed have a better idea of how to save the human race—in this way we acknowledge that the Messiah and Lord is coming into our midst in a way every bit as real as He did in old Jerusalem, and so we sing: *Benedictus qui venit in nomine Domini. Hosanna in excelsis.* And not just today, but every day, until He comes again in glory and even unto eternity—*in sæcula sæculorum. Amen.*

# PALM SUNDAY

## YEAR B

*Isaiah 50:4–7*
*Psalm 22*
*Philippians 2:6–11*
*Mark 14:1–15:47*

The Church calls this day by two names: Palm Sunday and Passion Sunday: The first, for victory—the name most people recognize (not surprisingly); the second, for suffering—the one most folks would sooner forget. But in the logic of the Church, which is likewise the divine Wisdom on the subject, these two names are complementary, not mutually exclusive or even paradoxical. The symbols of victory achieve their significance only in and through the Lord's enduring of His Passion. What are the lessons we can glean from this truth?

A marvelous tale is told about Marco Polo, the medieval traveler—of how he shared the story of Christ with the mighty men of Cathay. The Oriental noblemen were mesmerized by his account of the words and deeds of the Nazarene. They sat on the edges of their cushions as Polo spoke of the growing tension between Jesus and the religious authorities of His day. They drew on their daggers when he came to the betrayal. Breathless, they hung on his words as he described the details of the trial and the scene before Pilate. Finally, the Emperor himself could no longer stand the suspense, making him inquire:

"And did this Jesus of yours then call down fire from Heaven—and slay them?"

Understandably, it was a tense moment, with the atmosphere highly charged. Polo felt as though he held the salvation of all of China in his hands. "No," he replied quietly. "He was nailed to a cross and died between two thieves." In went the daggers and back went the listeners to their routine chores. To their minds, that was surely no way to prove that anyone was a son of the gods. Of course, it was the very same reception to that same message a millennium earlier that caused St. Paul to observe that the Cross was "a stumbling block to the Jews and folly to the Gentiles."

How did you react to the Passion narrative today? How will you react to it the rest of this Holy Week? How will you react to it the rest of your life?

Some people—good Christians among them—will simply shake their heads and echo the title of Rabbi Kushner's book, *Why Do Bad Things Happen to Good People?* But that reaction would be a mistake, because the Passion did not "happen" to Jesus. After discerning this as His heavenly Father's Will, He did not flee this eventuality; He did not grudgingly tolerate it; He actively and lovingly embraced it.

Others will be moved to question what kind of God, let alone Father, could demand this from His Son. But that, too, would be an erroneous response. God did not force His Son onto the cross; God did not require a pound of His dear Son's Flesh or a quart of His precious Blood. Nor can we even blame ancient Jews or Romans for this torturous experience. The Mystery of the Cross is best explained by a line I found recently on a poster in a Catholic grammar school library; scrawled in big, bold letters beneath the Calvary spectacle I found the wise words: "It was not the nails that held Him—but love!"

Yet others will be stirred to compassion. And that would be good, were it of the right brand. Compassion for the Lord in His sufferings can never be pity; one pities a poor, helpless puppy—not the Son of God. "Compassion" comes from the Latin words for "suffering with" Christ; in fact, this is the only appropriate response, because it will demonstrate our understanding of the Cross in His life, as well as in our own.

The dramatic reenactment of the Passion is intended by Mother Church to engage her children in their Lord's sufferings at the deepest possible level and to bring us to appreciate the insight of Monsignor Luigi Giussani, the founder of *Comunione e Liberazione*, who declared that "God saves man through man." In the Man Christ Jesus, the entire human race was redeemed—*in potentia*; the application of those merits, however, is a process that will continue until He comes in glory. How does it go on?

First of all, as you and I freely accept the benefits of His saving Death and Resurrection, responding to these unimaginable graces by living like saved and holy people. Secondly, the work of Redemption is carried on each and every time that we accept our share of the Cross—without grumbling, without doubting. St. Paul was fully conscious of this when he reminded his readers that we brothers and sisters of Jesus—members of "His Body the Church"—must fill up in our own bodies what is still lacking to the sufferings of Christ. That was not Pauline blasphemy; it is Christian theology at its best, for it acknowledges that the Passion of Christ is not complete until each of us identifies with it personally—in just the same manner as our Captain in the struggle. Thirdly, the Passion perdures and exercises its power whenever we believers attempt to lead others to know, love, and serve the Lord of Calvary. You and I have the privilege and duty of inviting others to come to the Savior's wounded side, there to be enlivened by the water and the blood that issue forth from His Sacred Heart.

Today's Epistle teaches us that Jesus became a slave—for our sake. And if He became a slave for us, can we do any less for Him and for every other person for whom He had become a slave? I think not. The great French poet and philosopher of the twentieth century, Charles Péguy, rhapsodized on this profound reality in his work "The Portal of the Mystery of Hope." Permit me to share it with you:

> He who loves becomes the slave of the one he
> loves.
> God did not care to evade this universal law.
> And by this love He becomes the slave of the
> sinner.
> The overturning of creation, it's creation upside-
> down,
> The Creator now depends upon His creature.

As the victim surrenders his hands to the
    executioner
So Jesus has abandoned Himself to us.
As the prisoner abandons himself to the prison
    guard,
So God has abandoned Himself to us.
As the least of the sinners was able to slap Jesus,
And it had to be so,
So the least of the sinners, a miserable, weak
    creature,
The tiniest of sinners is able to bring to failure,
    is able to bring to fulfillment
       A hope of God;
The tiniest of sinners is able to uncrown, is able to
    crown
       A hope of God;
And it's from us that God awaits
The crowning or the uncrowning of one of His
    hopes.

This holiest of weeks is given to us to determine our level of compassion; to allow us to show—by our lives—if we truly grasp how the palms and the Passion go together; to remind us of the one overriding hope that God has had for each of us from all eternity—the hope that we would share in His unbounded, faithful love forever.

# PALM SUNDAY

## YEAR C

*Isaiah 50:4–7*
*Psalm 22*
*Philippians 2:6–11*
*Luke 22:14–23:56*

If we consider the Passion narratives of the first three evangelists, known as the Synoptic writers, St. Luke's is not the longest, yet it contains more of our Lord's own words than do the others. Furthermore, it is St. Luke alone, the compassionate evangelist, who offers some tender details, on which we should meditate today.

Remember that, as our Lord prays in the Garden of Gethsemani, Luke tells us that in this hour of agony His sweat became like drops of blood falling to the ground. Picture, if you can, the anxiety, the intensity of our blessed Lord, and envision His holy Face, upon which the sweat had accumulated for the three years of His redemptive mission. And surely, He would soon shed every last drop of His most Precious Blood—for our salvation.

We might ask, "Did Jesus merely agonize in anticipation of His crucifixion and death, or did He agonize for all those who, down the centuries, would reject the cup of suffering He accepted and fail to pray with Him those humble words to the Father: 'Let not My will, but Yours be done.'"

But St. Luke notes yet another detail: "An angel came

and comforted Him." Is this not the same consolation offered to all of us who each day willingly deny ourselves, take up our personal crosses, and follow along our own road to Calvary? During these past forty days, we have received consolation in the Sacrament of Penance or, please God, will do so within the remaining days of this Holy Season. Hopefully, if we are not "sleeping from sorrow" like the Apostles, we will be present to receive, through those same Apostles, the consolation of the Blessed Eucharist and the consoling gift of the Sacred Priesthood on Holy Thursday. On Good Friday, the consolation of the "Wood of the Cross, on which hung the Savior of the World," will be unveiled for us. On Holy Saturday, at the Easter Vigil, in the darkness of the night, we shall be consoled by the warmth of the Sacred Fire and walk in the light of the Paschal Candle. And finally, on Easter morning, we shall be consoled as we gaze with faith upon the empty tomb and the statue of the Risen Christ.

St. Luke's detailed narrative also tells of how, after Peter's shameful denial and the triple cock-crow, Jesus gave Peter a powerful glance, one that moved him to heartfelt repentance. Certainly, this is the glance that Christ cast on us, through His Church, at the beginning of this Holy Season of Lent—one that we hope has moved us to greater prayer, fasting, almsgiving, penance, and conversion.

Only Luke describes how Jesus turned to the weeping women of Jerusalem, His Face clothed in sweat and blood. He prolongs His agony to stop and offer them a word of divine hope and consolation—although He really only gave them another cause for tears, as he reminded them of their own sins and those of their children. Ironically, however, once again Jesus' glance leads even apparently good women to deeper repentance, for they come to see that even their smallest sins are reason enough for Jesus to walk this *Via Dolorosa*.

Beyond that, St. Luke recalls that our divine Savior glances three times from the Cross. First, Jesus looks to Heaven and says: "Father, forgive them, for they know not what they do." Then, turning to the repentant thief, He assures him: "Amen, I say to you, this day you will be with Me in Paradise." Finally, gazing upon the heavens, He cries out with resignation: "Father, into Your hands I commend My Spirit."

Remember all this, my dear people, as you gaze upon the priest bearing aloft the Sacred Host, the Cross, and the Paschal Candle during the liturgies of this truly Holy Week. Remember that, like the sleeping Apostles, the weeping women, the petrified Peter, the angry crowd, and the good thief, it is only the gentle but piercing glance of the crucified and risen Savior that leads to repentance, forgiveness, and eternal salvation. And although today we resemble the crowd in their eagerness to wave palm branches at the Messiah's triumphant entry, may we not scatter later this week and throughout our lives like frightened sheep when the time comes for us to follow our Lord up the road to Calvary.

Do not shun the holy countenance of the Savior during this holiest of weeks; rather, gaze upon It with tender affection and compassion, and allow It to transform you.

# MONDAY

## HOLY WEEK

*Isaiah 42:1–7*
*Psalm 27*
*John 12:1–11*

The readings this week show us Jesus in His final days, and they point to many characteristics of His personality. Today's Servant Song of Isaiah presents God's Chosen One as a Person Who rules, gently, quietly, peacefully—and thus He fulfills His mission. As Christians, we share this mission "to open the eyes of the blind, to bring forth prisoners from confinement, and from the dungeon, those who live in darkness." How? By gently and peacefully following the example of our suffering Lord.

# TUESDAY

## HOLY WEEK

*Isaiah 49:1–6*
*Psalm 71*
*John 13:21–33, 36–38*

In the last hours, Jesus is not only tormented by the prospect of imminent death but also by infidelity within His own select group. Peter and Judas are sober reminders of the need for constant prayer if we are to remain true to our Christian vocation. As we share these final hours with Jesus, let us hope that our Lenten observance has strengthened us sufficiently to stand at the foot of the Cross with Mary and John and, somehow, to see through this agony to a future vindication.

# WEDNESDAY

## HOLY WEEK

*Isaiah 50:4–9a*
*Psalm 69*
*Matthew 26:14–25*

As the time gets closer, our hearts get heavier, and we find it more difficult to speak. Sorrow is always acutely experienced but seldom adequately expressed. And so it is with us Christians today; we wait and suffer with Jesus—in silence.

# SOLEMNITY OF ST. JOSEPH

## MARCH 19

*2 Samuel 7:4–5, 12–14, 16*
*Psalm 89*
*Romans 4:13, 16–18, 22*
*Mark 1:16, 18–21, 24* OR *Luke 2:41–51*

Joseph is a model for all believers; he acted according to God's commands, even though he could not understand them. Jesus also accepted His destiny as part of His Father's Will. In a short while, we will be entering into Christ's last hours with Him, and we will have to recall and *believe* that God is on that cross, as ludicrous as that may seem. And, at some unknown moment, we will be called upon to imitate the pattern of Our Lord's death in our own lives. For such times, let us pray for the faith of a Joseph, who saw in all things God's Will and His love.

# SOLEMNITY OF THE LORD'S ANNUNCIATION

## MARCH 25

*Isaiah 7:10–14*
*Psalm 40*
*Hebrews 10:4–10*
*Luke 1:26–38*

Today the Church's liturgy invites us to pause in our Lenten penances, to celebrate this great Solemnity of the Annunciation. And even though there is no penitential character about the feast, it really does fit in rather well with our Lenten observance.

Simply think of the kind of woman Mary must have been—full of faith, full of trust, full of love. Such virtues develop over a lifetime lived for Almighty God and other people. And that is exactly what we are trying to do during this holy season: Prepare ourselves to hear the Word of God and put it into practice. God can do great things, if we let Him: A virgin conceived; Jesus was raised from the dead. What do you want Him to do for you? The key is in preparation and cooperation.

# TRIDUUM AND EASTER

# HOLY THURSDAY

On only one day during the entire liturgical year does the Church specifically direct the priest as to what he should discuss in the homily, and that occasion is today's Mass of the Lord's Supper. The Roman Missal says that "the homily should explain the principal mysteries which are commemorated in this Mass: The institution of the Eucharist, the institution of the priesthood, and Christ's commandment of brotherly love." All three—Eucharist, priesthood, and Christian love—work together to form a unified understanding of what happened on this day nearly two thousand years ago.

If you are observant, you noticed when you came into church tonight that the tabernacle is empty. Why? For two reasons, really: First, to ensure that everyone receiving Holy Communion this evening does so from altar breads consecrated at this particular liturgical service, placing us at the Last Supper with Jesus and His chosen band. Second, and in some sense, even more important, to make us reflect on what life in the Church would be like without the Eucharistic Christ. How barren, how cold, how lifeless would our churches be if the Lord of the Eucharist were permanently absent, rather than truly present. Perhaps this insight explains the centrality of the tabernacle in our churches. Perhaps this realization helps us understand what makes us genuflect when we enter a Catholic church, not in mockery, like the soldiers during our Lord's Passion, but in adoration and thanksgiving and love. For Jesus Christ, Son of God and Son of Mary, the Second Person of the Blessed Trinity, comes into our midst in a unique and marvelous manner as the Church gathers to renew the sacrament and sacrifice that He bequeathed to her on this holy night. Imagine, the God in Whom and through Whom the universe was created comes among us and within us. My dear people, too many of us have become too accustomed to this simple fact of Catholic life; we need to be shaken out of our routine, in order to appreciate—as if for the first time—the true significance of it all.

The great American convert to the Catholic Faith Thomas Merton, at once an accomplished author and Trappist monk, describes in his autobiography, *The Seven Storey Mountain*, his First Holy Communion. As I share his reflections, think back on your own first encounter with the Jesus Who deigns and desires to come to us under the forms of bread and wine. Merton puts it thus:

I saw the raised Host—the silence and simplicity with which Christ once again triumphed, raised up, drawing all things to Himself—drawing me to Himself. . . . I was the only one at the altar rail. Heaven was entirely mine—that Heaven in which sharing makes no division or diminution. But this solitariness was a kind of reminder of the singleness with which this Christ, hidden in the small Host, was giving Himself for me, and to me, and, with Himself, the entire Godhead and Trinity—a great new increase of the power and grasp of their indwelling that had begun [in me] only a few minutes before at the [baptismal] font. . . . In the Temple of God that I had just become, the One Eternal and Pure Sacrifice was offered up to the God dwelling in me: The sacrifice of God to God, and me sacrificed together with God, incorporated in His incarnation. Christ born in me, a new Bethlehem, and sacrificed in me, His new Calvary, and risen in me: Offering me to the Father, in Himself, asking the Father, my Father and His, to receive me into His infinite and special love. . . .

What magnificent thoughts. Most of us could not fashion the words in so poetic and powerful a way, but most of us had a similar experience at our First Holy Communion. I still recall with devotion and emotion that momentous occasion in my life in 1957, kneeling at the altar rail of St. Rose's Church in Newark, New Jersey. I can yet remember even the exact spot where I knelt at that rail and how the months of study and preparation seemed as nothing in the awareness that the God Who had created both me and the universe was now coming to dwell within me in a new and wondrous manner. Having been baptized into Christ's Body, the Church, which is likewise His Bride, I was now being brought into a union even more close and more intimate than that of marriage: Through the Eucharist, Jesus and I would become one. How I trembled at the prospect for which I had waited so long, not from fear (because I was never trained to relate to God in that way) but from love and joy. The priest was only two children away from me, now one. Finally, he stood before me and, signing me with the Sacred Host, prayed, *"Corpus Domini nostri Jesu Christi custodiat animam tuam in vitam æternam"* [May the Body of our Lord Jesus Christ preserve your soul unto life eternal]. As I opened my mouth and pillowed Christ on my tongue, I knew I was entering upon a new mode of existence, destined for life eternal. And I am sure that my childhood recollection is not so different from anyone else's here tonight; we all need to recapture that enthusiasm, that innocence, that faith which brings us to appreciate precisely what the mystery of the Eucharist is in itself and for us. If we did understand what we do so regularly, how different we would be—no sloppy or thoughtless genuflections; no half-hearted liturgical participation; no unworthy and unprepared-for Communions; no arriving late and leaving early; no frivolous socializing in the presence of the One Whom the Sacred Heart Litany calls "the King and center of all hearts." Yes, my dear friends, we all need to ask our Lord on this holy night to grant us the grace to have a second honeymoon with Him Who, on the day of our First Holy Communion, became the Bridegroom of our souls.

Now the Church instructs me to reflect with you on a second matter, the holy priesthood. As many know from my own testimony, I wanted to be a priest from my first day in kindergarten, but that desire was ratified and solidified on the day of my First Holy Communion. So awesome was the experience of that occasion that I promised our Lord that I would be an instrument of His to enable others to know and share in the close and loving relationship I had just embarked upon. In so much of Western Europe and North America, we find ourselves short of priests. We are told by pollsters that this is so because celibacy is an impossible burden today, because the Church is out of step with the modern world, because young people are being offered many more attractive options in life. I disagree. The reason why we have fewer priestly vocations is that so few young people today have been introduced to the full mystery of the Eucharist. If they knew what happens in each celebration of the Eucharistic Sacrifice, we would have so many candidates that we would either be turning them away or building new seminaries year in and year out—as they are in Africa and Poland and Lithuania. Ask any seminarian what attracted him to the priesthood, and I daresay that you'll get the same basic answer—a love for Christ's Eucharist and a sincere desire to make that Presence available to the Church until the Lord comes again in glory. That is why the priesthood exists; we live for Christ and for you, our people. And regardless of the faults and failings and sins that may haunt us as weak, fallible men, if we do at least that much right in bringing you this sacrament of Christ's love, that love will cover a multitude of sins, as the First Epistle of Peter tells us. And because of this immense work of love, the Catholic people have always taken their priests into their hearts and homes, loving them as the fathers of this family of faith. While never blind to the weaknesses of their priests, they have nonetheless never ceased to love them and to pray for them. We priests here tonight pledge to you once more in this solemn hour and liturgy this one redeeming service; in return, we ask that you continue your saving prayer on our behalf. Priests and people, then, are united in a common desire for the Blessed Sacrament of the Eucharist.

Unity is our final consideration. The word "Eucharist" means "thanksgiving," but thanksgiving for what? Thanks for making us one with Christ, for sure, but also one with every other member of Christ's Church and, ultimately, in God's good time, with every other member of the human race. That unity or community is at the core of what it means to be a believer. As Catholics, we are not "Lone Rangers" in our journey back to the Father; no, we are pilgrims accompanied by Christ and by His entire Mystical Body, the Church. Holy Communion provides us with the necessary food for the pilgrimage, bringing us into unity with Christ and then with one another. That unity is expressed by what we profess with our lips and by the way we live our lives. In each offering of the Eucharistic Sacrifice, we note that we engage in this holy action "in union with" the Bishop of Rome and the local bishop. We believe what they teach because this is the Faith that "comes to us from the apostles." And because we believe in such things as the Trinity and the Incarnation and transubstantiation, we are called to live holy lives, different from the pagans around whom and among whom we find ourselves. The Eucharist challenges us to be different, and yes, that means being better than other people. That sense of difference should not make us arrogant or obnoxious; it should make us humble and grateful, because the only reason we are capable of being different is that the grace of Christ is given to us and is working within us, most especially because of our reception of Holy Communion. How much, then, should we love our Holy Father and the local bishop, who is Christ for us in the local church; how much, then, should we love one another, refusing to be party to hateful actions like gossip and slander and envy, which bring division and strife into the Body of Christ. When outsiders see Christians fighting among themselves, is it any wonder that they reject not just Christians but Christ Himself? The German proverb teaches that "a man is what he eats." If that is true, how Christ-like our conduct needs to be, how careful we must be to love all men, but especially those who belong to the household of the faith. Wars do not occur simply because mighty military powers decide to kill each other; wars begin when human beings fail to reflect the love of God in their daily lives—at home, at school, at work, in the parish community.

Once more, Thomas Merton can help us understand this point. He writes: "I knelt at the altar rail and on this first day of the Second World War received from the hand of the priest, Christ in the Host, the same Christ Who was being nailed again to the cross by the effect of my sins, and the sins of the whole selfish, stupid, idiotic world of men." Do you see how all three themes of our liturgy coalesce in that one scene? Holy Communion, the priest, the individual's relationship to other human beings.

On the first Holy Thursday, Christ the God-Man could see beyond His present moment to the end of time. He knew that our unity with Him and with one another required the gift of the Eucharist, which in turn called for the gift of the priesthood. In His great love, He graced His Church with those two sacraments. I beg you to bring that thought to mind as I hold the Sacred Host aloft tonight and say what is said in every Holy Communion: "Behold the Lamb of God! Behold Him Who takes away the sins of the world! Blessed are they who are called to the wedding feast of the Lamb." Blessed indeed.

# GOOD FRIDAY

Most people shrink from suffering. The Jesus we meet in today's Passion narrative marches boldly and resolutely toward it. The Scriptures tell us that Jesus learned obedience from what He suffered. What does the author of the Epistle to the Hebrews mean by that? The word *obedience* comes from the Latin word for "listening intently." Jesus listened intently to His Father's will and plan, and acted accordingly. The Son of God, having learned from His suffering, now teaches us—if we are willing to be educated in the school of the cross. The founder of the Passionists, St. Paul of the Cross, once remarked that we should go before the Crucified One more to listen than to speak. Why? Because wisdom comes from the wounds of Jesus. What are some lessons we can learn here today?

Wisdom comes from the wounds of Jesus, as we see powerful proof that God, in Christ, literally loved us to death. Entering into a relationship of love always involves risks, most especially the risk of rejection. Throughout salvation history God made overtures of love toward His people and was rather consistently rejected, yet He tried again in Christ His Son and then received the ultimate rejection—death. But we do not focus our attention so much on the rejection of the people as we do on the greatness of the love, so great that death itself had no power over it.

Wisdom comes from the wounds of Jesus as we realize that the wounded One is at one and the same time our healer. The jeering crowd at Calvary urged Him Who had saved others to save Himself. Little did they know that the blood and water that flowed from His wounded side would become the source of life-giving birth to the Church, which has continued Jesus' work of healing the wounds of sin and division ever since.

Wisdom comes from the wounds of Jesus as we discover that to reign best requires one to serve most. It is for this very reason that Jesus was never more the king than from the throne of His cross. It had to be more than Pilate's stubbornness that kept that mocking plaque proclaiming Jesus a king over His head; it had to be a part of God's eternal plan—in a sense, giving God the last laugh on people who still could not see how a servant could be a king.

Wisdom comes from the wounds of Jesus as we learn how to love completely and remain true to oneself and one's mission unto death. In one of His many parables, Jesus had observed that a good shepherd would be willing to lay down his life for his sheep. Good Friday proves how good our Shepherd is. During His life on earth, Jesus once told His listeners that those who were faithful to the end would hear the Father say to them: "Well done, good and faithful servant. Come, inherit the kingdom prepared for you from the foundation of the world." Jesus practiced what He preached. He was fidelity personified.

Wisdom comes from the wounds of Jesus as we are

taught how to believe in a loving Father when seemingly abandoned by Him. Someone once noted that Christianity is the only religion in which even God for a brief moment sounded like an atheist, as Jesus cried out from the cross, "My God, My God, why have You abandoned Me?" But if the Lord did not finish Psalm 22 aloud, we know that He surely completed its sentiments in His heart, as that psalm concludes on a note of confidence and absolute trust in God.

Christians, then, worship for all time a wounded healer. And we are not embarrassed or ashamed because, as Julian of Norwich put it, we do not really look on these as wounds but as honorable scars—tokens of victory and of love. And so it is that we come today to listen to the words of wisdom that come from our wounded healer—and yes, to adore Him.

# THE SEVEN LAST WORDS OF CHRIST

### 1.

### *"Father, forgive them."*

Significantly, the first of Christ's last words is: "Father, forgive them, for they know not what they do!" (Lk 23:24). Luke was not only a sensitive author; he also understood psychology long before it was a course for future teachers.

St. Luke saw the connection between a teacher's words and life. Therefore, the Jesus we meet in Luke's Gospel does not merely command prayer and teach prayer; we *see Him pray*.

Similarly, Luke's Jesus fashions parables on forgiveness, but, far more important, we observe Him put those parables into practice from the pulpit of His cross. In His humanity, Christ teaches the most powerful lesson on forgiveness—by forgiving.

All people desire the experience of forgiveness, so it comes as no surprise that every major religion offers that possibility. Christianity, however, makes the personal experience of it hinge on a believer's forgiveness of others: "Forgive us our trespasses—as we forgive those who trespass against us."

Having taught His disciples those words, Jesus now showed them a concrete application of the petition by *this* petition: "Father, forgive them," which presupposes that Christ the Man has already extended His forgiveness to His executioners and detractors.

What does it take to forgive? A unique mental attitude is required at the natural level; only an infusion of divine grace can elevate that sentiment to the supernatural level.

Only then do we perceive that forgiveness is not just an option or a luxury but a necessity.

Christian forgiveness is rooted in the notion of human solidarity, since we're all children of the one Father. Jesus was not a naïve Pollyanna, though; He knew what was in men's hearts (cf. Jn 2:25). And so He offers an additional motivation: the knowledge that our common humanity also provides us with another and baser form of solidarity—solidarity in the sin of the world, from Adam at the dawn of time to me in this particular time and place.

That, in turn, calls for a twofold acceptance: first, the awareness of the sinful condition of humanity (which isn't all that hard to discover or believe); and second, the awareness of our own personal sinfulness (which sometimes takes a lifetime to learn or at least to admit).

The Lord's Prayer seems to say, then, "If a supernatural love of neighbor doesn't move you to forgiveness, then remember your own sins and know that every member of the human family has the same basic needs, including forgiveness."

Jesus, Who never needed forgiveness, forgave readily, even enthusiastically. Like His ancestor Abraham, He was even willing to intercede for sinners (cf. Gen 18).

How different from most of us, who can dream up the most brilliant excuses for ourselves but simultaneously deny the most legitimate excuses of others.

Truly great people don't need to point an accusing finger at others; petty ones do. Being non-judgmental does not mean calling black white or evil good; it does entail giving others the benefit of the doubt, which Jesus does on Calvary. After all, how could they have knowingly crucified the King of the universe? No, *they know not what they do*, thank God!

In the same way, every follower of Christ is invited by Him to adopt a generous spirit in evaluating the motivations of those who cause us injury. Jesus goes so far as to command His disciples to ask for forgiveness in the same measure they are prepared to impart it: "Forgive us—as we forgive others." What a frightful thought for most of our race!

God forbid that He should take that petition literally! What does that mean in the practical order—stop reciting the Lord's Prayer? Well, maybe a moratorium on it until we demonstrate an openness to integrating its message into our daily life.

How might that occur? First, by examining personal patterns of forgiveness. Do I forgive grudgingly, or only when I stand to lose more by holding out, or to please another, or because I'm suffering more than my enemy? In other words, do I want peace and reconciliation for reasons of expediency? Or do I forgive because my love for God bids me to love all His children, even those who harm me?

Second, am I blessed with the ability to forget? So often people say, "I can forgive, but I can never forget what you've done." I would argue that the two go together. The inability to place injuries off center stage is an indication that all is not well. Humanly speaking, it is so psychologically damaging because it makes the "victim" remain so forever.

In His forgiveness, Jesus ceases to be a victim; on the contrary, He becomes the victor. The martyrs, from St. Stephen onward, have always understood that. Forget, and move on with the business of life.

As I heard a man's confession recently and had just uttered the prayer of absolution, the penitent thanked me and said, "Father, those words are the most beautiful words known to man!"

That's very true, but it's equally true that no one can claim them who is unprepared to extend them to others.

As the priest commingles the water and wine in the Mass, he prays, "May we come to share in the divinity of Christ, who humbled Himself to share in our humanity." How can that prayer become a reality? The adage says that "to err is human, but to forgive is divine."

In His final hours, Jesus launches out on the road of forgiveness, clearing the way for us to share and receive forgiveness—and blessings besides.

2.

*"This day you will be with Me in Paradise."*

So many sermons preached on this second word of Christ from the Cross revolve around the "good thief who stole Heaven." And so they often miss the point, because the focus is blurred.

St. Luke wants us to fix our gaze on two characters, but in proper order: first, the Speaker; second, the one addressed.

In His last moments on earth, Jesus makes a commitment with eternal consequences. As He hangs in agony, He hold out an offer that continues the pattern of His life; He claims thereby to have a unique entrée to everlasting life. In fact, He's dying for this very reason.

Therefore, we need to consider some alternatives about His identity: This convicted criminal is insane; He is the blasphemer He's accused of being; or He's the Son of God that He alleged Himself to be.

Luke believed the last alternative and wrote his Gospel to bring others to that same faith. We are the beneficiaries of that tradition. There is no other alternative for us, either.

Because Jesus *is* the Son of God, the Second Person of the Blessed Trinity, His promise to the good thief has significance. God is as good as His Word. The ancient Hebrews had a highly developed understanding of the word; any word was a part of the speaker, now with an independent existence. That applied equally to good words and bad words. Just think of poor old and blind Isaac deceived into blessing Jacob. However, once the word of blessing was uttered (ill-gotten as it was), it could not be recalled.

God's Word is as omnipotent as He, for through it the work of creation was accomplished: "By the word of the

Lord the heavens were made" (Ps 33:6). If God can create everything from nothing, He can save the good thief.

Now, this offer by Christ was not a special "one-day sale"; He gives the same opportunity to every one of the Father's adopted children in Baptism. The promise of salvation is nothing less than the promise of the Gospel. "This day" is a sign of the immediacy of the gift, so that we do not find ourselves waiting for the experience of justification, redemption, or salvation at the end of time; we receive it and live it "this day."

The battle for our souls was fought on Calvary. The devil lost, and so we won. It sounds so simple, too good to be true. Efforts to complicate the message and to condition its power fail to take God at His Word, which informs us that He wants all men to be saved (cf. 1 Tim 2:4).

Preachers who suggest that Dismas (as tradition speaks of him) "stole Heaven" do not do justice to the gratuity of salvation. For in a sense, we all "steal Heaven" because none of us is worthy to behold the face of God. The dying thief did, however, have certain qualities that provided fertile soil for God's Word to take root.

First of all, he had the tremendous gift of self-knowledge. Some people go through life believing their own public-relations material. The thief, on the other hand, was bitterly aware of his own sinfulness: "We deserve it, after all. We are only paying the price for what we've done" (Lk 24:41).

What extraordinary honesty and maturity! No blame shunted off onto bad parental example or a deprived childhood. With the Psalmist, he could say: "For I acknowledge my offense, and my sin is before me always: 'Against you only have I sinned and done what is evil in your sight'—That you might be justified in your sentence, vindicated when you condemn" (Ps 51:5–6).

Second, Dismas did not measure himself by the evil of others: "You know, we live in a society where 'everyone' steals and cheats, if only given the opportunity. I just got caught." Rather, he took as his yardstick the holiness of God: "This man has done nothing wrong" (Lk 24:41). His words and underlying attitude reflect those of another Lucan figure who could say, "O God, be merciful to me, a sinner" (cf. Lk 24:41).

Third, all of his behavior on the cross proves him to be a man open to the workings of grace. Therefore, it does not surprise us to hear him plead: "Jesus, remember me when you enter upon your reign" (Lk 23:42). He was already to hear the promise: "This day you will be with me in paradise" (Lk 23:43).

What does all of this have to do with us, most of whom are not thieves and none of whom would ever be crucified for the crime anyway? We've been allowed by Luke to eavesdrop on a conversation that teaches valuable lessons on how we are saved. We learn that God can save us and wants to do so. We discover that He is willing to wipe clean the whole slate. What do we have to do in return? Believe God and live in His love.

"You mean I don't have to do anything?" comes the incredulous reply. I didn't say that—I said we must believe God, taking Him at His word. That realization makes the entire faith–works controversy of the Reformation a meaningless discussion. We are not saved *by* good works or *without* them. We are saved by faith, a faith that necessarily expresses itself in love. And that's how the experience of salvation can be known right now—with no waiting for a day of judgment. As St. Thérèse of Lisieux put it, "All the way to Heaven is Heaven."

A believer doesn't try to rack up "brownie points," maneuvering God into a corner, "forcing" Him to grant salvation through human manipulation. A heartfelt believer trusts God's promise and loves Him as the only appropriate response. What lover does not desire intensely to do good for the beloved? But this is surely not as a means of gaining an advantage in the relationship, for that would be neither love, nor trust, nor faith.

No, the person of faith stands in the tradition of Dismas, who was prepared to hear the promise of the Gospel and, as a result, began a whole line of Christian "thieves" who have "stolen" Heaven ever since.

### 3.
### *"Woman, behold your son."*

The most important "deals" in history were struck on Calvary through some truly admirable exchanges, always redounding to the benefit of the individual believer. This is especially true in our present reflection.

The Mother of Christ is given into the care of the beloved disciple. On the surface, it seems that Jesus is merely ensuring His Mother's well-being after His death. A closer look, however, suggests that the *disciple* is the one who's really being cared for.

Throughout the New Testament we find references to Mary. In fact, at every key juncture in our Lord's life, we see Mary on the horizon. When God began His plan for our redemption, He sent to Nazareth an angel, who hailed a woman as "highly favored" or "full of grace" to be the human partner in this divine task (cf. Lk 1:28).

When the Babe was born in Bethlehem, He came forth into our world not from Heaven but from the womb of the Virgin Mary (cf. Lk 2:7). As the Child was presented to the Almighty in the Temple at Jerusalem on the fortieth day, the old prophet Simeon singled out His Mother Mary for special mention as a woman destined to be the Mother of Sorrows (cf. Lk 2:35). Twelve years later, after another Temple visit, the Boy Jesus returned with His Mother and foster father to Nazareth and was subject to them (cf. Lk 2:51).

It was Mary who prodded her Son into action at Cana to work His first miracle, launching Him on His public ministry (cf. Jn 2:3f.). And it was Mary who stood by His side at the foot of the cross and was given to John as the Mother of the Church (cf. Jn 19:25f.), to use Paul VI's beautiful phrase. Finally, as the Church was waiting to be born in the Upper Room, while the disciples prayed for the Pentecost gift of the Spirit, Luke tells us that Mary was in their midst (cf. Acts 1:14).

Three passages of Johannine origin should be pondered in greater depth, two of them already noted in passing. Most serious Scripture commentators agree that

John has the most highly developed theology and literary style of all New Testament writers. The structure of John's Gospel is a masterpiece in which even the arrangement of material and the introduction of certain people advance the theological agenda.

For example, the deliberately unnamed "beloved disciple" is generally regarded to stand as a symbol for the ideal Christian in every age who stays with Jesus to the end—and beyond. Another figure of prominence, however, is the Mother of the Lord, who appears only twice (unnamed also and simply addressed by her Son as "woman"—to establish the connection between her and the original woman, the mother of all the living, in Genesis).

The Lord's earthly ministry ended on Calvary with the beloved disciple and the "woman" brought into a unique relationship with each other by the dying Christ. The beloved disciple, representative of every committed Christian, in that moment was given the Mother of Christ to be his own mother. The physical maternity of Mary was thus extended to include now a spiritual motherhood of the Church, her Son's brothers and sisters. Just as she brought Christ's physical body into the world, now she would play a role on behalf of His mystical Body, the Church. Mary did not ask for this role; it was nothing less than her divine Son's dying wish for her and for His Church.

The theme of the woman who is the Mother of the Church reaches a climax in Revelation 12. Readers are brought up short as they try to unravel the symbolism. Is the woman laboring to give birth Mary or the Church?

The author of Revelation was so skillful a writer that both interpretations are possible, and both are probably intended. Catholics see the parallels as more than a happy coincidence, for the roles of Mary and the Church intersect at many points.

The class of 1954 of Seton Hall University erected a shrine to the Blessed Mother as their graduation gift during that Marian Year. As a young seminarian, passing it daily more than a decade later, I was continually struck by the simple, manly, yet profound devotion of the inscription: *Filii ad Matrem* (Sons to the Mother). That captures the essence of a healthy and scripturally based regard for the Mother of God, because it links together all the necessary ingredients: the Son, the Mother, and the Son's Church, which shares His Mother.

When the disciple agreed to "take her into his care," he did himself (and all who would succeed him as disciples) a far greater favor than he did her. In the plan of Providence, his action became the occasion for joining inseparably the Son with His brothers and sisters, all of whom can lay claim to a common Mother, "who occupies a place in the Church which is the highest after Christ and also closest to us" (*Lumen Gentium*, no. 54).

4.
*"My God, My God, why have You forsaken Me?"*

"Father, forgive them. . . . This day you will be with Me in Paradise. . . . Woman, behold your son." The first three words all have an air of the regal and divine about them.

In fact, they can sound more like utterances of an impassive Greek god on Mount Olympus than the anguished cries of Calvary's Suffering Servant.

But wait, Jesus' final sermon is not over yet. Now comes the fourth word, in which His sacred humanity shines with such brilliance. The Son of Man, identifying *with* man, speaks the haunting word that has echoed down the centuries: "Why?"

Why evil? Why suffering? Why death? Why do bad things happen to good people? Why does God seem so far removed from it all? The intriguing observation has been made that in this one line of Christ, for a twinkling of an eye, even God sounded like an atheist.

St. Paul, in his turn, asks a question, too. He presents it rhetorically: "He who did not spare His own Son but handed Him over for us all, how will He not also give us everything else along with Him?" (Rom 8:32).

The problem of evil is resolved only in reference to the mystery of the cross. Christian theology has a very balanced view of suffering. We need never seek it out and may actually pray for deliverance: "Father, if You are willing, take this cup away from Me" (Lk 22:42).

However, when it *does* come, the cross must finally be embraced: "Still, not My will but Yours be done" (Lk 22:42).

When faced with suffering, a human being has several options. The first is to shrink from it by escaping into drugs, sex, sleep, or some other reality-denying technique. The second is to accept the pain with bitter resignation, reminiscent of an earlier generation of existentialists such as Sartre and Camus. The third is to see in suffering an invitation to growth (at the psychological level) and participation in the Lord's Paschal Mystery (at the faith level). The first two postures are unacceptable for a Christian. So we need to consider the implications of the third.

One who believes in the God of the Bible knows the meaning of Divine Providence: namely, that our lives are always in the hands of a loving, omnipotent Father. That helps us see that "nothing is going to happen to me today that God and I, together, won't be able to handle."

Easier said than done? Jesus led the way. He showed us how suffering can be humanizing and divinizing at the same time. Chapters 4 and 5 of the Epistle to the Hebrews show this clearly as we read that, in Christ, "we have a great high priest who has passed through the heavens" (Heb 4:14), first having "offered prayers and supplications with loud cries and tears to [God]" (Heb 5:7).

Most important, "Son though He was, He learned obedience from what He suffered; and when He was made perfect, He became the source of eternal salvation for all who obey Him" (Heb 5:8–9). Thus, Jesus is our model in suffering.

Although the Old Testament presents us with a provident and immanent God, suffering does not become bearable and meaningful (even for a holy man like Job) until God Himself endures it in His Son. Therefore, while it's true that Christ dies for us (in the sense of atoning for our sins), it's equally true that He did not mean to eliminate suffering and death as a personal experience for His brothers and sisters.

From that vantage point, we must conclude that Jesus did not die in our stead but, through His own Death and Resurrection, taught us *how* to die—and rise.

In the sixties, it was fashionable to suggest that Christ's recitation of Psalm 22 on Calvary showed torment and despair. Better exegesis, however, suggests a man of faith who chooses a psalm tailor-made to His needs. First, this prayer acknowledges the existential situation: fear, confusion, anxiety. But then comes an awareness that God is present in this traumatic hour, and *that* becomes the foundation for a new perspective of hope.

This attitude never denies the reality of pain, but it does allow pain to be considered in the light of a future of vindication and joy. And so our Lord can say: "My God, My God, why have You forsaken Me?"

Nevertheless, immediately He is impelled to follow up on that with sentiments that culminate (in the psalm) with lines such as these: "I will proclaim Your name to my brethren. . . . Let the coming generation be told of the Lord that they may proclaim to a people yet to be born the justice He has shown." (*Post crucem, lucem*; "After the cross, the light.")

In Christ, the Second Person of the Trinity, God tackled head-on the problem of evil and even that of His own seeming remoteness. For God was, in Christ, reconciling the world to Himself, as St. Paul teaches. The cross, bearing the Suffering Servant, still asks the question—in the name of all humanity—"My God, My God, why have You forsaken Me?"

That same symbol also answers the question.

## 5.
### "I thirst!"

Irony and misunderstanding dot the landscape of St. John's Gospel.

The Johannine Jesus makes many remarks with huge symbolic importance only to have His obtuse audience become befuddled or, worse yet, grasp a meaning our Lord never intended.

This is clearly the case as Christ speaks His fifth word: "I am thirsty" (Jn 19:28).

For *what* does He thirst? Surely not for the narcotic mentioned in Mark 15:36. No, Jesus thirsts for more important things, but the Cross separates outsiders from the disciples. So, while non-believers do not comprehend His meaning, the faithful need only recall the words He spoke to them so often and so tenderly, especially the very night before. Thus they are ready to hear and understand these cryptic words, for to them "has been given a knowledge of the mysteries of the reign of God, but it has not been given to others" (Mt 13:11).

Jesus *thirsts* "to drink the cup the Father has given" Him (Jn 18:11). The *kenosis*, or self-emptying, so movingly described by St. Paul (cf. Phil 2:6–11), will not be fully achieved until the chalice of pain is emptied, drunk willingly and lovingly by the Father's Son. Once He begins the cup of obedience and suffering, He thirsts until the divine Will is accomplished. No half-hearted activity will do. The redemption of the world requires the same total abandon as the world's creation. The Spirit, too, will be lavish in the world's sanctification. Too much love has been poured out already to destroy it with a niggardly response now.

He *thirsts* to return to His heavenly Father. "I have given you glory on earth by finishing the work you gave me to do. Do you now, Father, give me glory at your side, a glory I had with you before the world began" (Jn 17:6). Of course, He and the Father are one (cf Jn 14:10f.), a unity not broken by the divine condescension in the mystery of the Incarnation. In a sense, His desire to return to the Father's right hand is motivated by the same altruism that first promoted the Incarnation and the Paschal Mystery itself.

He *thirsts* to complete the salvation of the world. His obedience, manifested in His Passion, needs to be sealed with the last drop of His Blood. His Father, in turn, will receive this sacrifice, sealing it with the Resurrection. And so, "it is much better for you if I go. If I fail to go, the Paraclete will never come to you, whereas if I go, I will send him to you" (Jn 16:7). And how will this salvation be completed? "I am indeed going to prepare a place for you, and then I shall come back to take you with me, that where I am you also may be" (Jn 14:3).

He *thirsts* to satiate us: "No one who believes in me shall ever thirst" (Jn 6:35). How strange that the source of living water (cf. Jn 7:38) should be thirsty, but He is, because He cannot be the font of eternal life until He has encountered death. In that moment, from His wounded side, flow out water and blood (cf. Jn 19:34), symbols of the sacramental life of the Church—Baptism and Eucharist, by which we are washed clean. Only in knowing thirst can He assure us that we will never thirst; only in dying can He destroy our death. Are we face to face with a contradiction or a paradox? Our answer reveals whether we belong to the world or to Christ. "For my flesh is real food and my blood is real drink. The man who feeds on my flesh and drinks my blood remains in me and I in him" (Jn 6:55).

During His earthly life and ministry, the Lord declared: "Blessed are they who hunger and thirst for holiness; they shall have their fill" (Mt 5:6). He was now on the brink of beholding the fulfillment of one of His own promises. The English poet Christopher Marlowe realized the "transferability" of it all, capturing the essence so beautifully: "See, see, Christ's blood streams in the firmament. One drop will save my soul, half a drop, oh my Christ."

It is precisely this reality that causes us to echo the Lord's "I thirst" until we have our fill with Him in the Kingdom He is preparing for us.

### 6.
### *"It is consummated."*

Translation is risky because it always involves some interpretation. So how is this sixth word of Christ on the cross (Jn 19:30) properly rendered into English: "It is finished" (as in "done," "over with"); "it is completed" (with a less fatalistic ring to it); or, "it is consummated" (in the sense of "brought to fulfillment")?

The correct choice requires a knowledge of the total Gospel of John, to which we must now turn.

The Johannine Jesus is wholly focused on His *hour*—the moment of glory. It cannot be hastened, as He had to remind His Mother: "My hour has not yet come" (Jn 2:4). Nor can or should it be forestalled: "The hour has come for the Son of Man to be glorified. . . . My soul is troubled now, yet what should I say—Father, save Me from this hour? But it was for this that I came to this hour. Father, glorify Your name" (Jn 12:23, 27–28).

Now, if most people were asked when Jesus' hour of glory began, they would probably say Easter morning. But John would disagree. The Lord, according to this Evangelist, began His hour of glory in His Passion, when He freely consented to the Father's plan for Him.

The Jesus we meet in John is the pre-existent Word (Jn 1:1–14)—always in control of His own destiny, never the helpless victim of either envious Jewish authorities or sadistic Roman soldiers. Death comes when He is ready, and not a minute sooner:

"The Father loves me for this: that I lay down my life to take it up again. No one takes it from me; I lay it down freely. I have power to lay it down, and I have power to take it up again" (Jn 10:17–18).

And so it is that Jesus *announces* (even *proclaims*) that the hour of His death has come, proving correct the ironic inscription over His head (see Jn 19:19). He is, in fact, never more a king than from the throne of His cross. In His death, the work of salvation is finished or, as the original Greek implies, the end or purpose is accomplished.

No morbid preoccupation with death here, for death (and especially *this* death) is the gateway to life. No room for the *Angst* of the existentialists of another era. Death is not the end, as common parlance understands it: death is The End, as Aristotle and Aquinas would have us ponder the word—the goal toward which reality struggles for fulfillment. It is in the light of this truth that Jesus' assertion makes the most sense: "And I—once I am lifted up from earth—will draw all men to myself" (Jn 12:32).

Dying, however, is not an end in itself. In the very act of dying, Jesus did one thing more—He "delivered over His spirit" (Jn 19:30). It is significant that John does not say that He "gave up" His spirit but "delivered over" (as in "gave forth").

Thus, we inquire, What is meant by "spirit"? Surely a play on words is intended, for spirit means "life principle" or "breath," but also spirit as in "Holy Spirit." Interestingly, it is only in "giving up" His own life principle that He can "give over" the Holy Spirit.

To whom is that spirit delivered? First of all, His earthly life is given over to the Father, Who seals it all with the Resurrection. Second, in fulfillment of John 7:39, He gives His Spirit to the faithful remnant, Mary and John, at the foot of the cross. Which is to say that He

144

gives His spirit to *us*, His Church, represented in glory's hour by the Church's Mother and the Church's first son.

That deliverance of the Spirit is achieved proleptically here, by way of a sure promise, only fully actualized after the Resurrection. However, time does not matter; in fact, eternity has taken over in the hour of glory, so that everything coalesces into a marvelous unity: Death, Resurrection, communication of the Spirit, birth of the Church.

Ignominy and triumph meet at the crossroads of Calvary in the hour of glory. The Savior knows this, and that is why He can declare so majestically: "It is consummated."

## 7.
### *"Into Your hands I commend My spirit"*

The Word Incarnate utters His last sentence, and in doing so, every last word takes on a special significance. In the act of dying, the God-Man teaches His brothers and sisters in the human family how to die. What is the final lesson?

Jesus died resigned to the Will of the One Who sent Him. However, we shouldn't see this as passivity; it's an *active* resignation, which sums up His entire life: "As a man lives, so shall he die."

Death is hard for anyone to face, but American culture has a particular dread of it. Our funeral customs speak volumes.

We refuse to use the words "death" or "dead" or "die"; we dress people up to look as though they're ready to host a party from their coffins; we say weird things, like "Doesn't she look wonderful?" All this suggests more than a desire to be tactful: It's a denial of reality.

Few humans beings ever look forward to death. Or, as one seminary professor used to put it: "Gentlemen, I know that Heaven is our true home, but I'm not the least bit homesick." Believe it or not, that's a healthy Christian attitude.

Modern man, however, has an excessive fear of death —and usually with good reason. Materialism has replaced faith as the motive force in society. The result: a smothering kind of despair.

Take the secular peace movement. No one has spoken more forcefully about war than the popes of the twentieth century, and especially John Paul II. But a Pontiff's style and content are so very different from non-Christian activists' because the former's vision is not earthbound—realizing as he does that, even in the best possible scenario, "Here we have no lasting city; we are seeking one which is to come" (Heb 13:14).

Human life is good and beautiful, as the great Fulton Sheen knew when he declared week after week that "life is worth living," but more compelling goods (e.g., testimony to the truth of the Gospel) can call for the relinquishing of that good (e.g., the death of Jesus Himself, subsequently embraced by the martyrs).

As we listen to the dying Savior, two words draw our attention: "*Father*, into *Thy* hands I commend my spirit."

"Father" and "Thy" are the keys to the mystery of death. Jesus, in His humanity, does not rely on His own resources but casts His cares upon His heavenly Father, the Abba ("Papa") in Whom He encouraged His disciples to have complete trust.

His heart is thus other-directed or, better, Other-directed toward the One "who was able to save Him from death" (Heb 5:7).

With eyes fixed on Jesus (cf. Heb 3:1), then, Christians ponder what they need in death. They are three: the grace of perseverance, the grace of final repentance, and the grace of a happy death.

As a seminarian, I used to visit an old nun in her community's infirmary. She concluded each meeting by saying: "Please pray that I have the gift of final perseverance." That request always caused me to wonder, "If *you* don't persevere, who will?" But one day she explained that remaining faithful to Christ never got easier and in some ways got more arduous as the years passed.

She had heeded the warning of St. Paul: "Let anyone who thinks he is standing upright watch out lest he fall!" (1 Cor 10:12). Mary and John at the foot of the Cross are the models of loyalty to Christ to the bitter end. The gift of perseverance is the basis of our hope, which "will not leave us disappointed" (Rom 5:5).

Each day Christians ask the Mother of the Church to "pray for us sinners now and at the hour of our death." Which means that we acknowledge ourselves as sinners, yet are confident of receiving the grace of final repentance, since the Mother of Mercy Incarnate has our deaths enfolded in her prayers to her divine Son.

The present AIDS crisis has caused me to reflect on God's plan, especially as I have helped some of these patients in their reconciliation with the Church. As catastrophic as AIDS is, it has one unbounded blessing for people of faith: It assures its victims of the opportunity to turn to God for forgiveness and spiritual healing. For them, death does not come "like a thief in the night."

But all people need the intercession of the Church for this great grace; most of us likewise need the Church's prayers *after* death as we undergo that process of purification which readies us to behold God face to face. Therefore, the Mass of Christian Burial (and, in fact, all Masses and prayers for the dead) takes on a huge importance.

So often contemporary funeral liturgies devolve into canonization ceremonies, as we're assured that the deceased "is now in Heaven praying for us." Wrong: We are there precisely to pray for the *deceased*. This concern with ultimate realities—the last things—is what unites a Church seemingly scattered in Heaven, in Purgatory, and on earth. The "communion of saints" prays that each of its members faces the moment of death in a way meriting eternal life.

Such a gift then leads to that most blessed thing of all—the grace of a happy death. Several years ago I received an early morning call to the hospital to bring Viaticum for a cancer patient I had attended the entire summer. Always thoughtful to a fault, she had restrained her family from contacting a priest during the night, lest he lose sleep. Upon my arrival, the woman stirred herself to prepare for her final encounter with the Eucharist.

As I placed the Host on her tongue, she smiled, swallowed, and died. Her son looked at me and said, "Father, that's all she was waiting for all night."

What a holy death! What a calming effect it had on her entire family! What a powerful and unforgettable witness she had offered! A *holy* death ensures a *happy* death because our eyes are "fixed on Jesus."

Thinking about death—our own death—should not be an exercise in morbidity but a truly positive opportunity. Alphonsus Liguori, author of the classic "Way of the Cross," provides ample food for thought in his reflection for the Fifth Station. It has within it all the serenity of Jesus' serenity in His final moments and thus recommends itself to our thoughts and as a guide for our actions—perennially.

And so we are encouraged to say—and to mean:

"My beloved Jesus, I will not refuse the cross, as the Cyrenian did; I accept it, I embrace it. I accept in particular the death You have destined for me; with all the pains that may accompany it; I unite it to your Death, I offer it to You. You have died for love of me; I will die for love of You, and to please You. Help me by your grace. I love You, Jesus, my love; I repent of ever having offended You. Never permit me to offend You again. Grant that I may love You always; and then do with me what you will."

# EASTER VIGIL

The Liturgy of this most holy night is nearly self-explanatory; in fact, the Early Church composed it precisely so that she could teach the summary of the entire Christian Faith in one fell swoop to those ready to be baptized, confirmed, and communicated at this "mother of all vigils": the powerful service of light, with its lovely and moving *Exsultet*; the refresher course in salvation history as we moved through the Old Testament texts; the welcome chanting of the *Gloria*; the solemn intonation of the *Alleluia* for the first time in more than six weeks; within a few minutes, the reassuring invocation of all the saints to be with us at the reception of catechumens into the Body of Christ in the Holy Eucharist, as well as our own renewal of baptismal promises.

Holy Saturday is the deadest day of the Church's year, but Christ was not dead today; the Creed tells us He spent this day going to the underworld to share the good news of redemption with the souls of the just who had died before His coming. One charming and most ancient homily for this occasion depicts Jesus "descending into hell" and preaching, first of all, to Adam, encouraging him to leave Hades and enter into the glory of the Resurrection. The words put into our Lord's mouth take Old Testament symbols and events and show how they are fulfilled in the Risen Christ, Who desires to share His new life with all. Let a few lines suffice:

Jesus says to Adam: "I am your God, Who for your sake have become your Son. Out of love for you and for your descendants, I now by My own authority command all who are held in bondage to come forth, all who are in darkness to be enlightened, all who are sleeping to arise. I order you, O sleeper, to awake. I did not create you to be held a prisoner in hell. Rise from the dead, for I am the life of the dead. Rise up, work of My hands, you who were created in My image. Rise, let us leave this place, for you are in Me and I am in you; together we form only one person, and we cannot be separated."

In truth, all the signs and symbols of the Easter Vigil Liturgy speak volumes, rendering my own words almost unnecessary. However, I would like to call your attention to one small but important detail from tonight's Gospel that could get lost in the shuffle of such a heavy bombardment of beauty and ritual; it goes along with the conversation of our Lord with old Adam. St. Luke tells us that the holy women went to the Lord's tomb to complete the burial rites and found that they couldn't because God had a better idea, namely, that the death of His Son should not be sealed but reversed—in a glorious resurrection. What is interesting is how the angels greet the women: "Why do you search for the living among the dead?" I would like to reflect on that line for a bit, because the action of those women perfectly summarizes the way we humans go about things on a regular basis; we are always looking for God, for life, for happiness, for fulfillment in the wrong places. Let me give you a few examples.

—We think money and material possessions are essential to human living, forgetting that even Howard Hughes died a broken, lonely man and that Leona Helmsley may actually die in prison as a result of greed. "Why do you search for the living One among the dead?"

—Jesus Christ teaches us that a permanent, exclusive relationship in Christian marriage—with no artificial contraception, no divorce and remarriage, no adultery, no fornication—is the only way to experience true marital bliss as the Creator planned it from the beginning. And people still express amazement that AIDS is a reality, that children's lives are destroyed because of their parents' infidelity, that spouses themselves are psychologically damaged. "Why do you search for the living One among the dead?"

—Our culture has been given over to immediate self-gratification of all needs, epitomized in the addiction to drugs, sex, and alcohol, in addition to abortions of convenience. Yet how many still don't get the message and come to understand that those who possess Jesus Christ and are possessed by Him do not need outside stimulants; Christ exhilarates from within the soul of His disciples. "Why do you search for the living One among the dead?"

—People have no time for God and religion. The holiest week of the Church's year finds all too many churches half-empty as supposedly good Catholics shop, go to movies, and watch television—just like all the other pagans of the land. But then they wonder why their lives are empty and not blessed by God in the most profound ways, and why falling asleep before the television is the best image for their hollow existences. "Why do you search for the living One among the dead?"

This list of sad, useless, contemporary efforts to reach ultimate happiness could go on, but I think you get the point. Everyone wants the fullness of life and joy, but so few are looking in the right places. In fact, they insist on going down all the dead-end streets, where people think they can discover life, only to find themselves grossly disappointed once again. Like those early hearers of the story of the Resurrection, many in our society today dismiss all this "God talk" as so much "nonsense," refusing to believe. But their refusal hurts only them. Tonight we thank Almighty God for the gift of faith and for the fact that He has taken us by the hand in Baptism and led us out of our enslavement to the world, the flesh, and the Devil into His true light and freedom. Like our father Adam, we are re-created into the image of God, Who alone holds the key to all true human longing for life, love, and joy.

The Risen Christ ends His discourse with Adam in a manner that applies to us as Adam's children. Let the Risen King have the last word:

Rise, let us leave this place. The enemy led you
out of the earthly paradise. I will not restore you

to that paradise, but I will enthrone you in Heaven. I forbade you the tree that was only a symbol of life, but see, I Who am Life itself am now one with you. . . . The bridal chamber is adorned, the banquet is ready, the eternal dwelling places are prepared, the treasure houses of all good things lie open. The Kingdom of Heaven has been prepared for you from all eternity.

# EASTER SUNDAY

If fear of the unknown is the most common phobia, and if death is the greatest unknown quantity in human existence, then I think it is safe to say that the fear of death is the greatest obstacle to living a genuinely happy and fulfilling life. At the same time, we know that during His earthly life Jesus assured us: "I have come that you might have life and have it to the full." Then, having said that, what did He do? He died. Strange, but therein lies the answer to the riddle of human existence. By His Death, our Lord reversed the downward spiral of human history, that downward trend set into motion by sinful Adam. Christ, the new Adam, confronts head-on the two-headed monster of sin and death by taking upon Himself our sins and by undergoing the experience of death.

The English poet Richard Crashaw reflected on this phenomenon in this way:

Christ when He died
Deceived the cross,
And on death's side
Threw all the loss:
The captive world awak'd and found
The prisoners loose, the jailor bound.

O dear and sweet dispute
'Twixt death's and love's far different fruit,

Different as far
As antidote and poisons are:
By the first fatal Tree
Both life and liberty
Were sold and slain,
By this they both look up, and live again.

O strange and mysterious strife,
Of open death and hidden life:
When on the cross my King did bleed,
Life seemed to die, Death died indeed.

Now, what was the reaction of those first witnesses to the Resurrection? Actually, we have to backtrack a bit and discover that even Jesus' closest friends were not expecting His Resurrection. They had been willing to concede to sin and death the ultimate victory by allowing Christ to stay in the grave. And so we find the women going to the tomb to complete the burial rites for their dear, dead friend. However, they did not find Him because they were looking for Him in the wrong place—a tomb—instead of seeking Him in the world He had just redeemed, the world where he had already begun His reign as Lord of life.

That is why the angel needs to remind those women that their actions are foolish, even if well-intentioned, because they are looking for the living among the dead. Those women, you see, in spite of their closeness to Jesus, had forgotten or perhaps even had stopped believing in His promise of eternal life. Therefore, they lost hope—that absolutely indispensable virtue for living a fully human and fully Christian life. Interestingly enough, neither the women nor the apostles needed to seek out the Risen Christ; He sought them out, the Scriptures tell us. The critical question for us, living two thousand years later, is: "Where might we find the Risen Christ today?" Or better, "Where might He show Himself to us?"

The Risen Christ reveals Himself to us in the Sacred Scriptures, for God's Word is, we are told, "living and effective, sharper than any two-edged sword." That record of faith gives us life, inspiring us to lead godly lives, motivating and challenging us to respond to God's overtures of love wholeheartedly and enthusiastically.

The Risen Christ reveals Himself to us through His Church, which is the sure guide to salvation as we go our pilgrim way back to the Father. Before His return to the Father, the Risen Lord promised His apostles and their successors that He would be with them until the end of time. By heeding the Holy Father and the bishops teaching in union with him, we Catholics receive the consolation of the truth of the Gospel in all its fullness, which is to say that we possess Christ and allow Him to possess us.

The Risen Christ reveals Himself to us through the sacraments. Was it any accident that in the last days of His earthly life and ministry our Lord began the sacramental life of the Church, and then continued to offer sacramental ways of encountering Him after His Resurrection? No accident, but the divine plan saw to it that

157

in just over fifty days the Scriptures give us evidence of the beginnings of five sacraments: Baptism, Holy Eucharist, Holy Orders, Penance, and Confirmation. In this way the Risen Lord shares with us His own risen life, preparing us for an eternal encounter with Him. How fortunate we are to have the foretaste and promise of Heaven right here on earth!

The Risen Christ reveals Himself to us in the lives of believers who live a truly moral life, "a new life," as St. Paul puts it, seeking "things above rather than things on earth." The new life shines forth in people who refuse to be mastered by the spirit of this godless age. They conform to Christ and not to the world. They give priority to God in their lives by weekly attendance at Sunday Mass, which gives them the strength to live like disciples of the Risen One. Therefore, sins of materialism, fornication, adultery, abortion, artificial contraception, divorce and remarriage—all sins very close to the heart of our society, these sins they avoid, but if they fall, they come to a forgiving, merciful Lord in the Sacrament of Penance, Who once again raises them up to the life worthy of a Christian.

The Risen Christ reveals Himself in the lives of Christian witnesses, who share the good news of God's love with enthusiasm and conviction, like those first witnesses of His Resurrection. And the result is that many more people are invited to share in the banquet of life that Christ has promised. And they will accept the invitation not because of the cleverness of our arguments but because of the depth of our faith and love.

The Risen Christ reveals Himself through hopeful people, who are not weighed down by the problems of this world, whether they be the threat of nuclear destruction, or poverty, or hunger, or disease. These hopeful people are not unconcerned about these human problems nor are they uninvolved, but their concern and involvement occur at a different level because they are able to see beyond the present reality to understand the meaning of Christ's declaration: "I have conquered the world!" And so every human difficulty has been taken up into the Lord's own Paschal Mystery and has been transformed, so that we view it in the light of Christ's Easter victory, and that is our reason for hope—and never despair.

At the Easter Liturgy, you are invited to renew the promises of your Baptism, for it was precisely in that sacrament Christ first shared with you His promise and gift of eternal life. Through Baptism you died with Christ to sin and death and rose with Him to newness of life. So why fear an enemy like death—an enemy that has already lost the battle? The poet Crashaw was right: We, the prisoners, have been loosed, while death, the jailor, has been bound. We know that this is true because the victorious and risen Lord has shown Himself plainly to us in so many convincing ways, and continues to do so.

The Paschal victory of Jesus Christ is ours for the asking. He has made the down-payment; He has, in fact, paid the price in full. We have only to claim the prize by joining our voices—and our lives—to those of the angels and saints as they sing before the throne of the Lamb the hymn of our eternal Easter:

> The strife is o'er; the battle done;
> The victory of life is won;
> The song of triumph has begun: Alleluia!
>
> The pow'rs of death have done their worst;
> But Christ their legions has dispersed;
> Let shouts of holy joy outburst: Alleluia!

To which we respond, "Amen, Alleluia indeed!"